Options and Agency

John T. Maier

Options and Agency

palgrave
macmillan

John T. Maier
Cambridge, MA, USA

ISBN 978-3-031-10242-4   ISBN 978-3-031-10243-1   (eBook)
https://doi.org/10.1007/978-3-031-10243-1

© The Editor(s) (if applicable) and The Author(s), under exclusive licence to Springer Nature
Switzerland AG 2022
This work is subject to copyright. All rights are solely and exclusively licensed by the Publisher, whether
the whole or part of the material is concerned, specifically the rights of translation, reprinting, reuse of
illustrations, recitation, broadcasting, reproduction on microfilms or in any other physical way, and
transmission or information storage and retrieval, electronic adaptation, computer software, or by similar
or dissimilar methodology now known or hereafter developed.
The use of general descriptive names, registered names, trademarks, service marks, etc. in this publication
does not imply, even in the absence of a specific statement, that such names are exempt from the relevant
protective laws and regulations and therefore free for general use.
The publisher, the authors, and the editors are safe to assume that the advice and information in this book
are believed to be true and accurate at the date of publication. Neither the publisher nor the authors or
the editors give a warranty, expressed or implied, with respect to the material contained herein or for any
errors or omissions that may have been made. The publisher remains neutral with regard to jurisdictional
claims in published maps and institutional affiliations.

Cover illustration: Jiale Tan

This Palgrave Macmillan imprint is published by the registered company Springer Nature Switzerland AG.
The registered company address is: Gewerbestrasse 11, 6330 Cham, Switzerland

Acknowledgements

I initially became interested in the questions addressed here during my first year of graduate work at Princeton, and I would like to thank many people there—especially my advisor, Gideon Rosen—for their patience and indulgence as I worked out my thoughts. I subsequently had the opportunity to develop these ideas further during several postdoctoral years in Australia and the UK. I would especially like to thank David Chalmers and Huw Price, my supervisors for those positions, for their philosophical guidance as well as the funding that supported me during that time. I continued to work on these topics as a faculty member at Peking University, where I benefited greatly from discussions with my colleagues and students.

Many additional colleagues have been supportive of my work and this project, and the following have been especially so: Miri Albahari, Xuhui Hu, Michael Nelson, and Barbara Vetter. I am also grateful for the help of my editor, Brendan George, and an anonymous reader for this press. Thanks to all of them, and to the many other people who have supported and inspired me over the last few years.

Contents

1	Foundations	1
2	The Simplicity of Options	17
3	The Analysis of Ability	41
4	The Active and Passive Powers	67
5	A Picture of Agentive Possibility	99
6	Against Reconciliation	115
7	Simple Compatibilism	133
	Afterword: Of Agents and Objects	151
	Bibliography	165
	Index	167

Introduction: The Philosophy of Agency

One of the distinctive features of a human life, as opposed to the natural history of a planet or of an iceberg, is how much it is characterized by things not done, or by invitations that have been declined. To be a lawyer is typically to be someone who has considered and declined several other career paths, and to be married to one person to be someone who has had the opportunity to not marry, or often to have married someone else. In this respect the life of an agent, unlike the history of a mere object, is characterized in part negatively, in terms of what that agent has not done as well as what that agent has done. This negative description of an agent does not show up in newspaper obituaries or even in biographies, but it looms large in the accounts we give of one another, and most of all in the accounts we give of ourselves.

When it is reflected in sentiment, this aspect of human life is the proper object of regret. Regret is a reaction to opportunities declined that, had they been taken, might have made one's life much better, or at least different, than it might have otherwise been. There is also a positive counterpart of regret, which curiously seems to lack a name in English, wherein one reflects on one's good fortune in having made exactly the choices that one has made, instead of the apparently worse ones which

x   Introduction: The Philosophy of Agency

seemed to be available.[1] In this respect our emotional life, as well as our intellectual one, is played out against a backdrop of possibilities, of things that could have been done.

The way in which an agent's life is bound up with possibility, and the way in which regret is a characteristic sentiment of agency, bear emphasis. For this is a book about the nature of agency. And a reader who has thought about agency through the lens of the recent analytic tradition in the philosophy of agency, a tradition to which this book is a contribution, might be apt to miss these fundamental aspects of agency.

Consider the very name of the discipline. It is typical to refer to the field that I am calling the philosophy of agency instead as the 'philosophy of action.' But action is just one aspect of agency and, as we have just said, not always the most important aspect. To refer to the philosophy of agency as the philosophy of action would be like referring to the philosophy of mind as the philosophy of thought, or like referring to the philosophy of language as the philosophy of utterance. These misnomers conflate a specific manifestation (action, thought, utterance) with the philosophical genus that they manifest (agency, mind, language). It is appropriate to refer to the field in terms of the genus itself, which is the proper object of philosophical attention.

This is not, I think, a terminological accident. The focus on action at the expense of other aspects of agency reflects the actualist bias of work in the analytic philosophy of agency, most of all the great work of Donald Davidson, and most of all Davidson (1980, Essay 1). This brief work has been far-reaching in its impact, and we are still just beginning to take its proper measure. That essay set itself the question: what is it for an event to be an action? It answered that an event is an action just in case it has a certain causal history, namely if it is caused in the right way by a certain belief and desire. Setting aside certain concerns about the details of this account, not least questions about how to understand 'the right way,' this account is plausible enough, and deeply elegant.

This account also had the effect of undermining all those who thought that actions were somehow outside of the causal order, because they

---

[1] This is roughly the kind of attitude that R. Jay Wallace, in his extended meditation on these themes (Wallace, 2013), refers to as 'affirmation.'

admitted of a certain kind of explanation, namely an explanation by reasons as opposed to an explanation by causes.[2] I follow Davidson in taking this opposition to be a false one. When I turn on the light and illuminate the room, my action is nothing but a causal happening, setting off still further causal happenings, all of them subsumed under the force, ultimately, of natural law.

Yet to say that this shows that agency is simply a causal process is to make the ground-level mistake that, I am arguing, characterizes the Davidsonian tradition. It is to focus on the actual at the expense of the possible, and to conceive of agency as in the first place a series of actions. But I have suggested that agency is far more than that, and a philosophical account that neglects that—one that takes the philosophy of action to exhaust the philosophy of agency—is an account that cannot help but be fundamentally incomplete.

Incidentally, the argument here is not to be confused with those authors who complain that Davidson leaves out the agent because he fails to accommodate the way in which the agent herself, as opposed to her beliefs and desires, gets into the story of action.[3] Here the objection is that a proper account of the natural order needs to somewhat include agents intervening on the world, for that is an irreducible part of what happens. I am sympathetic with Davidson (Davidson, 1980, Essay 3) that this proposal is a non-starter. The best explanation of the actual course of history, including the actions of agents, will ultimately include only the fundamental physical constituents. For Davidson, these were causal relations among events. For other philosophers, causation might be superseded by something still more fundamental, such as the laws. Yet I agree with Davidson that we do not need to introduce agents themselves into the explanation of actions to give a proper account of them. When I say that Davidsonian philosophy of action tends to leave out the philosophy of agency, I mean something rather different from this.

What I mean instead is this. To be an agent is to be someone who acts. But it is also, and more generally, to be someone who can act in many ways,

---

[2] This view appears to have been in the very atmosphere of philosophy in the years preceding Davidson's article, but a particularly sharp defense is Hampshire (1959).

[3] This complaint is raised with great force, and without appeal to the kind of agent causation described in the text, in Velleman (1992). As will become clear, my own conception of what has gone wrong in Davidson is quite different from Velleman's.

and who declines to act in most of those ways. Agency is in the first place a confrontation with possibility. This is not only the most fundamental aspect of agency, but the most difficult to reconcile with the fact that we are part of the natural order. Our acts are rightly construed as casual or anyhow nomically governed processes. But how do we construe our innumerable possibilities for action with the fact that we are, in the end, natural beings, composed of atoms and subject to the physical laws, as well as products of natural selection subject to all its constraints? These are questions that remain even after we have given a causal theory of action.[4]

This is to say that the actualist tendencies that are foundational to Davidson's work[5] have tended, given the wide influence of that work, to make the philosophy of agency appear to be a narrower and more tractable enterprise than it really is. The problem of giving an account of what we do is important and interesting. But the central problem in the philosophy of agency—the hard problem, as it were (Chalmers, 1996)—is to give an account of everything that we do not do, but could. It is that problem to which the discussion that follows will be addressed.

There is a further reason for the focus on action at the expense of the negative and merely possible aspects of agency. This is distinct from Davidson's focus on action and its causal history. Indeed, this tendency lies wholly outside the Davidsonian program in the philosophy of agency, and may indeed be thought of as a complementary tradition in the recent philosophy of agency. This is the approach to questions of agency that focuses, above all, on questions of moral responsibility.

The philosophy of agency, at least as it has been practiced in recent anglophone philosophy, has tended to be less sharply distinguished from moral philosophy than are areas such as the philosophies of mind and of language. This is understandable. Agents intervene in the world and thereby affect one another for good or for ill, and one of the driving forces to understanding agency is to understand, and perhaps evaluate

---

[4] Davidson's main confrontation with this kind of question occurs in Davidson (1980, Essay 4), and is a particular kind of 'conditional analysis' of agentive possibility. In Chap. 2, I will explain why this kind of account fails.

[5] Davidson's reluctance to engage questions about modality has roots that extend well beyond the topic of agency. The semantic program expounded in Davidson (1984) is notable for its studious avoidance of modal devices.

these effects. In fact, this moral tendency in the philosophy of agency has tended to be focused, still more narrowly, on a specific set of questions in moral philosophy: these are questions specifically about moral responsibility and the conditions under which agents are morally responsible.

It is a vital question in the recent history of philosophy to understand why precisely moral responsibility has taken on this prominence within the philosophy of agency more broadly. Here, however, I am concerned not with the etiology of this tendency but with its effects. If one is canvassing agency with an eye towards the assignment and justification of moral responsibility, then one will tend to focus, in the first place, on the things that agents do. For agents are morally responsible in the first place, for their actions, and more specifically for the harms that they bring about. We can consider the question of moral responsibility for omissions, and indeed this is a rich and vexed topic.[6] But in terms of both frequency and relative priority, it is acts (as opposed to omissions) that tend to be taken as basic for the assignment of moral responsibility. Therefore, a focus on moral responsibility will tend to be another source of actualist bias in the philosophy of agency.[7]

This methodological tendency is reflected in the moral psychology that governs many recent discussions of agency. Following Strawson (1962), many philosophers have taken the moral sentiments to be foundational to a proper understanding of moral responsibility. Above I endorsed the significance of sentiment for the understanding of agency, and most of all the centrality of regret to our conception of ourselves. Yet regret is often marginal in much recent work in the philosophy of agency, for regret is not constitutively connected to questions of moral responsibility, or even to moral questions at all. Instead, and again following the influence of Strawson, it is resentment that has figured most centrally.

---

[6] See Clarke (2014) for a thorough discussion of this topic, as well as the connection between omissions and agency more broadly.

[7] This is not the only bias that tends to foreground questions of moral responsibility in discussions of agency. Another is an anthropocentric bias, neglecting all the non-human agents who are also not, on most accounts, morally responsible for what they do. Any close tie between moral responsibility and agency founders on the observation, developed with great force in Steward (2012), that chimpanzees and otters are agents as well.

Resentment recasts, in the sentimental mode, the intellectual tendency already highlighted above. What agents typically resent are the acts of others, particularly that the acts that have caused them harm. It is certainly possible to resent someone for an omission, but this is the degenerate case. It is in the first place other people's actions towards us that we resent, and accordingly an orientation towards resentment—an orientation which has shaped much philosophy under the considerable influence of Strawson's great essay—will tend to be another pressure for narrowing the philosophy of agency proper down to the more constrained questions posed by the philosophy of action.

It bears emphasizing, as suggested above, that this is a different pressure from that exerted by Davidson. The idea that moral responsibility should be central to the philosophy of agency is utterly alien to a Davidsonian approach. Questions of responsibility and resentment simply do not arise in Davidson's foundational work on the philosophy of agency. Davidson articulates a vision on which we can understand and adjudicate the basic questions about agency—action, intention, freedom, and much else—without even mentioning questions of moral responsibility, which arise downstream if at all.

The vision of Strawson and those who follow him is altogether different. It is one on which we begin with moral responsibility, and with the morally valanced intricacies of human life more generally, in constructing our account of what it is to be an agent. I do not want to force a choice between these perspectives (though, as will become clear, the methodology of this discussion will hew much more closely to Davidson's vision, on this question at least). I simply want to point out that these two quite opposed but deeply influential tendencies in the recent philosophy of agency converge on a crucial, but mistaken, idea: the idea that the philosophy of agency should begin with action, or with what is actual, as opposed to the vast array of acts that are, for any agent, possible.

The tendency in recent anglophone philosophy, then, has been to focus on the philosophy of action at the expense of the larger questions involved in the philosophy of agency proper. This line of thinking has at least two distinct sources. One of these is the focus on the causal etiology of action foregrounded in Davidson and his successors. The other is the focus on moral responsibility and specifically on resentment foregrounded in

Strawson and his successors. None of this is to deny the significance of the questions raised in these discussions, but only to underscore their relative narrowness and to emphasize the breadth of questions that they leave open.

What then would a philosophy of agency look like, distinct from the philosophy of action? There are three dimensions on which this distinction might be made.

First, there is the significance of the negative, in addition to the positive, aspects of agency. Whereas philosophy of action tends to attend to the causal history of what we do, our omissions loom just as large in our practical consciousness, and demand to be included in an account of agency. Sometimes it is suggested that omissions might be regarded as a special case of action, but there are convincing arguments (Clarke, 2014) that this is not so. The negative aspect of agency is a topic in its own right.

Second, there is the significance of the future, as opposed to the past, aspects of agency. Both the causal theory of action and the theory of moral responsibility are essentially backward-looking in their concerns. They look to the history of a certain event to determine whether certain conditions are met, namely the conditions on being an intentional act, or being an act for which one is morally responsible. Yet agency is fundamentally oriented towards the future, in the mental states that characterize it, most of all the mental state of intention (Bratman, 1987), but also in non-psychological modes of relating to time (Thompson, 2008). A philosophy of agency that does justice to the temporal orientation of agents is one that is concerned with the future as much, if not more, as it is with the past.

Third, there is the significance of the possible, as opposed to the actual. In a way this last item subsumes the prior two. It is not simply our inactions or our future actions that are significant to us. It is those inactions and future actions that are possible for us that are the ones that matter. An account of agency therefore owes us, most of all, an account of this sense of possibility. This is a question on which discussions of agency in the anglophone tradition, in recent decades, have been curiously quiet.[8]

---

[8] There has of course been extensive discussion of the metaphysics of modality generally in recent analytic philosophy, building on the possible worlds tradition in modal logic, a discussion that reaches its apex in Lewis (1986b). But this tradition tends to neglect the issue of agentive modality. In Chap. 2, I will argue that a possible worlds framework is inadequate as an account of agentive modality.

xvi   Introduction: The Philosophy of Agency

This has been an unfortunate tendency. A philosophy of agency that deserves the name should include, at a minimum, an account of agentive possibility.

I have emphasized the relatively recent and local aspects of these narrowing tendencies in the philosophy of agency. Accordingly, when one broadens one philosophical perspective, one encounters philosophers with a broader conception of their topic. Especially relevant here is the work of Jean-Paul Sartre (Sartre, 1956). Indeed, those aspects of agency that I have criticized the recent anglophone tradition for neglecting—negativity, futurity, and possibility—are precisely, for Sartre, the defining features of agency. In Sartrean terms, the recent anglophone philosophy of agency is not really a philosophy of agency at all—it is a philosophy of facticity.

Why is the Sartrean tradition more alive to these aspects of agency? It is not merely a historical accident, though it is I think partly that: the brilliant interventions of Davidson and Strawson set the agenda for philosophers in a way that was not easy to overcome. It is also, I think, because of the fundamentally phenomenological mode of Sartre's work, as opposed to the explanatory orientation that one finds in Davidson and even in Strawson. For these aspects of agency are not ones that show up prominently if one is attempting to explain and to evaluate the behavior of agents. For those purposes, an account that focuses on the actual and historical aspects of agency may, at least at first approximation, be sufficient. But if one is seeking an account that incorporates also the perspective of the agent herself, not merely as a subjective feature but as an element in the very account of what it is to be an agent, then one will inevitably be drawn to these three aspects of agency. From the point of view of an agent, it is precisely the various future acts that she could perform, but likely will not, that are most salient.

We need not go to the phenomenological tradition, however, to appreciate the significance of these aspects of the philosophical agency. We can hew closely, if we wish, to recent anglophone philosophy. For, as noted above, the actualist tendencies in the philosophy of agency are not shared by cognate areas of philosophy, notably the philosophy of mind and the philosophy of language. Both areas of philosophy demonstrate a lively preoccupation with the broad range of possible thoughts and utterances, as well as the significance of the first-personal point of view in giving an adequate account of their subject matters.

One way of appreciating this asymmetry is in thinking about the fundamental ontology of these domains of philosophy. The philosophies of mind and language, as they have developed in the analytic tradition, have taken as their fundamental object the proposition. There is an ongoing debate about what propositions are and what exactly their place is in a final theory, but there is general agreement that they are the proper objects of inquiry, in large part because their generality allows them to capture the merely possible aspects of thought and talk (as opposed, for instance, to utterances). Propositions have not had a comparable role to play in the philosophy of agency. If there is an ontological object that plays the role of the proposition in the anglophone philosophy of agency, it is the event. But the event is inadequate to capture the essentially negative and non-actual aspects of agency. This yields a question which at this point in the discussion must remain unanswered: what objects play in the philosophy of agency the role that propositions play in the philosophy of mind and language?[9]

A philosophy of agency that deserves the name will therefore be one that is properly integrated with the philosophies of language and mind. It will not be subject to the curious balkanization that has characterized the anglophone philosophy of action in the recent decades, where the field is marked by set problems (for instance, the evaluation of the kinds of cases proposed in Frankfurt (1969) and the endless variations upon them) that seem curiously disconnected from larger philosophical programs. The philosophy of agency would be a part of philosophy proper again.

It is helpful to consider how the tendencies identified here have affected the discussion of specific philosophical problems. Foremost among these is the problem of free will. As I will argue in what follows, there is in fact not one problem here but an entire family of problems, or perhaps a family of related anxieties. The actualist tendencies involved in a focus on action at the expense of agency have the effect of focusing philosophical

---

[9] Below I will introduce the core idea of this discussion, the idea of an option. It is options, I will eventually argue, that are the basic objects of agency, and which therefore are fit to play this role.

xviii   Introduction: The Philosophy of Agency

attention on just one of these problems, instead of the many different and perhaps deeper in the intellectual vicinity.

Here is one way of presenting the problem of free will. Consider an agent who performs an act, which is typically one we wish to blame someone for: for example, embezzling some money from a charity. We trace the history of this agent's act and find, in its antecedents, influential events that were outside of the agent's control. Perhaps the agent had a brain lesion that led him to lose his sense of right and wrong. Perhaps, further back, the agent was raised in a household where theft for one's own advantage was tacitly encouraged. Or perhaps the world is deterministic and the initial conditions of the universe, conjoined with the laws of nature, imply that the agent would embezzle the money at exactly the time and in exactly the way he did.

These historical antecedents appear to show that, even if the agent's embezzling was an action (satisfying, for example, the conditions of the causal theory of action), it was nonetheless not up to the agent, and was not one with respect to which he had free will. From this it is claimed to follow—either straightaway or via some additional premises—that the agent was not morally responsible for what he did. This seems to undermine our initial moral judgment about this agent. And since something like this argument seems to apply to all the things that agents do—that is, since all actions have their antecedents something outside the agent's control, at least if the world is indeed deterministic—it appears to follow that all our judgments of blameworthiness for wrongdoing are undermined.

I do not so much want to solve this problem, whatever exactly it would mean to do that, as to notice its presuppositions. This way of presenting the problem of free will—which is predominant in many recent philosophical discussions—is shaped by precisely the biases identified above. It focuses on what an agent has done, rather than what an agent has not done. It focuses on the actual series of events, rather than possible alternatives. And it focuses altogether on the past, including the distant past, rather than what lies in the agent's future.

This framing of the problem has given rise to an entire literature. On the one hand there are those, such as Fischer and Ravizza (1998), who hold that the actual sequence of events leading up to an agent's act can

Introduction: The Philosophy of Agency   xix

suffice to make her responsible for that act, even in a deterministic world. On the other there are those, such as Strawson (1994), who hold that this is impossible, and that the very possibility of tracing all of our acts to the distant past undermines the very possibility of moral responsibility.

This way of understanding the problem of free will has become so much part of the philosophical education in certain quarters that it can be hard for some to even conceive of an alternative to it. But there is an altogether different way of conceiving of the problem, one on which it is in the first place a problem about agency, rather than about action.

To begin, take up the point of view of an agent. The presentation of the free will problem given above begins from a third-personal point of view, where one looks at an agent from the outside and attempts to determine whether he is responsible for what he has done. But it is possible instead, and arguably more natural, to consider things from the agent's point of view.[10] When considered from this point of view, the issue seems to be the following. I am confronted by a vast range of alternatives, among which it seems I must choose. Yet—considering the very same arguments canvassed above—it can appear that my act will be the consequence of past events that are beyond my control. So, I do not really confront a range of alternatives after all. There is exactly one thing that I will do, though I may not yet know what it is. The appearance of freedom is an illusion.

This presentation of the problem has several differences from the earlier presentation, in addition to its more phenomenological orientation. It is concerned just as much with what an agent does not do as with what an agent does—the argument does not even need to specify the agent's act for the argument to be stated. It is concerned in the first place with what is (purportedly) possible for the agent, rather than with what the agent does. Finally, although it appeals to the history of action in the development of the argument, its upshot is concerned with the future. The upshot of this argument is not that we are regrettably unable to blame anyone for what they have done. It is rather that our conception of our futures as full of possibility is a mistake. There is simply one path for

---

[10] Compare Velleman (1989), which draws a useful distinction between the 'conceptual' and the 'phenomenological' problem of freedom.

xx   Introduction: The Philosophy of Agency

each of us, and our pretensions to the contrary are just as futile as the movements of the servant who would escape to Samarra.[11]

Notice that this problem is not really a problem about action at all. For any act that one performs, it may well be brought about in the proper way, without interference or influence. The issue is rather that there is exactly one act that one can perform, against our presumption that at any moment each of us can perform many acts. This formulation of the free will problem puts the emphasis on 'free': freedom is a fundamentally modal condition, in the sense that it involves the availability of several distinct possibilities. This formulation of the free will problem holds that, at least if the world has a certain structure, this modal condition is not met.

Notice also that this problem is not really a problem about moral responsibility either. The issue is not in the first place whether one is morally responsible for what one ends up doing. It is rather whether our first-personal presentation of ourselves as having multiple possibilities for action is veridical. Accordingly, this problem arises in everyday contexts just as much as it does in morally fraught ones.[12] When I am shopping for pasta at the grocery store, it appears that there are several varieties of pasta available and that I can choose any one of them. On this development of the problem of free will, this appearance is false: there is at most one that I can choose. Moral responsibility is not typically at issue in such trivial cases, but the same basic metaphysical issue nonetheless arises.

We can, if we wish, make this problem a problem about moral responsibility. We might articulate a principle that links having various acts

---

[11] *There was a merchant in Bagdad who sent his servant to market to buy provisions and in a little while the servant came back, white and trembling, and said, Master, just now when I was in the marketplace I was jostled by a woman in the crowd and when I turned I saw it was Death that jostled me. She looked at me and made a threatening gesture. Now, lend me your horse, and I will ride away from this city and avoid my fate. I will go to Samarra and there Death will not find me. The merchant lent him his horse, and the servant mounted it, and he dug his spurs in its flanks and as fast as the horse could gallop he went. Then the merchant went down to the marketplace and he saw me standing in the crowd and he came to me and said, Why did you make a threatening gesture to my servant when you saw him this morning? That was not a threatening gesture, I said, it was only a start of surprise. I was astonished to see him in Bagdad, for I had an appointment with him tonight in Samarra* (O'Hara, 1934; attributed to Somerset Maugham).

[12] Contrast the view of van Inwagen (1989), who holds that freedom arises only in certain morally significant situations. The view here is that the nature of agency is basically the same across moral and non-moral contexts.

available to an agent with that agent's being morally responsible for what she does. The 'principle of alternative possibilities' that was questioned in Frankfurt (1969) is exactly such a principle.[13] But this problem is not in the first place a problem about moral responsibility. It is in the first place a purported conflict between the way an agent experiences the world and the way the world in fact is.[14]

I do not want to quibble over which of these problems deserves the name the 'problem of free will.' That is a verbal question. As noted above, there are several distinct problems that go under this heading, each of them with some purchase in the history of modern philosophy. My point rather concerns the unfortunate tendencies of a single-minded focus on action and its history in the recent philosophy of agency. That focus induces certain forms of myopia, not least a tendency to obscure the way in which the problem of free will can present itself phenomenologically, and independently of worries about moral responsibility. One effect of broadening our conception of the philosophy of agency and its concerns is that it makes this problem available, once more, for philosophical reflection.

Finally, I want to consider a question to which much of this book will be devoted: what is the proper ontology and semantics for a philosophy of agency? Davidson gives an extended answer to this question for the philosophy of action. Actions are simply a kind of events, and the semantics of action sentences is to be told in terms of quantification over events (Davidson, 1980, Essay 6). But this does not suffice for the many things that an agent does not do. What are the acts that an agent does not perform? And what is the semantics for the claim that the agent is able to perform these acts? Neither of these questions can be answered by events, for there are no events here to play the required role.[15]

---

[13] The principle is stated as follows: 'A person is morally responsible for what he has done only if he could have done otherwise' (Frankfurt, 1969, p. 829).

[14] In this respect, the problem of free will has analogies to the problem of external world skepticism. In fact, the problem of free will has an epistemic dimension even when we approach it from the point of view of moral responsibility, as argued in Maier (2014).

[15] It is natural to appeal here to 'merely possible' events. These are natural denizens of a possible worlds framework, but not of Davidson's own more austere ontology.

xxii   Introduction: The Philosophy of Agency

What is needed is something more general, something that is present just as much when the agent does not act as when the agent does. Earlier I asked: what is fit to play the role in the philosophy of agency that propositions play in the philosophy of mind and language? I want to close by proposing an answer to this question.

It is options, I will argue, that play this role. An agent's options are all those acts that she can perform, including both those that she performs and those that she does not. Claims about what an agent is able to do are to be told, in a way that I will explain, in terms of quantification over options. The ontology and semantics for the philosophy of agency proper is to be given in terms of options.

Options are generally not regarded as a central topic in the philosophy of agency, at least under that name.[16] But this is a consequence of precisely the philosophical biases criticized in the foregoing. I have argued that recent tendencies in the anglophone philosophy of agency—as opposed to tendencies in the broader philosophy of mind and action, as well as to the phenomenological tradition in the philosophy of agency— have tended to focus philosophical attention on the positive, on the actual, and on the past, at the expense of the negative, the possible, and the future. Each of these biases has naturally led to a neglect of options.

Begin with the bias towards the positive. If one is concerned with what agents do, rather than with what they do not do, then one can, at least with some success, disregard agents' options. If an agent raises her arm, then this might naturally be regarded as an event, and one does not need to introduce options into one's ontology in order to describe it or to give a semantics for sentences reporting it. This demand arises only when one considers further questions, such as capturing the contrast between the way in which the agent raised her arm and all the other ways in which she might have raised it. It is this is partly these sorts of considerations that have led some philosophers to countenance an ontology of ways in their account of practical agency.[17] I think we should instead countenance an

---

[16] The cognate notion of ability is a central topic in the theory of agency (Maier, 2020). As I will argue in Chap. 3, talk of ability is ultimately to be explicated in terms of options.

[17] To take one influential example, ways are central to the semantics for knowhow defended in Stanley and Williamson (2001).

Introduction: The Philosophy of Agency   xxiii

ontology of options: the agent has a plurality of options involving her raising her arm, but she exercised exactly one of these.

Consider then the bias towards the actual. If one is concerned with what agents do, as opposed to what they can do, then one can also disregard options. A philosophy that is wholly concerned with what agents actually do, as opposed to the many acts that are open to them, may never find it forced to invoke options in either its metaphysics or its semantics. Indeed, this is essentially the story of the Davidsonian program in the philosophy of agency.[18] But this simply reveals the limitations of this kind of program. As soon as one considers the variety of acts that agents do not perform, one is forced to reckon with the question of agentive modality, and this is a question that leads us in short course to options.

Consider finally the bias towards the past. If one is concerned with what agents have done, as opposed to what they might do, then one can also disregard options. Indeed, the idea that the central problem in the philosophy of agency is one of articulating the kind of causal history that constitutes an action tends precisely to elide the significance of options. For options may not be needed in a historical account of why an agent has acted as she has. But they are definitely needed in an account of the various acts that an agent might, in the future, perform.

Once these biases are correct, we recognize the need for an ontology of options. Or, more accurately, when we take up the natural view of agency—on which the possible looms as large as the actual—options come into view on their own. Options are as readily apparent, within the philosophy of agency, as is action itself.

The foregoing considerations present something like a non-constructive argument for options, in the sense in which that term is used in mathematics. That is, they present an argument that there must be something in our philosophy of agency that is oriented towards the negative, the possible, and the future, and argue that options are the things that play that role. But they do not demonstratively introduce options themselves. That is, they do not point to an agent's options in specific cases, or explain

---

[18] As noted earlier, Davidson does attempt to extend his program to capturing the possible aspects of agency in Davidson (1980, Essay 4), but this attempt, I will argue, is ultimately unsuccessful.

xxiv   Introduction: The Philosophy of Agency

what principles are true of options. That constructive task—say what options are—will be begun in Chap. 1.

To return to the place where we began, the point of these remarks is not simply to engage in some boundary-marking within philosophy. It is to give a philosophical account of agency that does subject to its subject matter, which is nothing less than agency itself. And agency, as I have said, is concerned as much with what is left undone as with what is done.

The idea that the philosophy of agency should be primarily concerned with giving an account of agency might seem too platitudinous to mention. But curiously, this platitude has not always been accepted, even once we waive the issue of whether action or agency is the proper focus of philosophical attention. For work in this area of philosophy has characteristically been motivated (focusing, again, on the recent anglophone tradition) by questions external to agency itself.

In one recent philosophical tradition, represented by Davidson, the problem of agency is really a problem about explanation. Davidson held that causation was the 'cement of the universe' (Davidson, 1980, Introduction), and that all explanation could be regarded as causal explanation.[19] Agency appeared to seem to many to fall outside this framework, since an agent's act of raising her hand seemed to be explained by her reasons (say, to alert someone nearby) rather than by any causes. It was precisely this that seemed to mark the difference between acts and mere events, such as an arm spasm, which were admitted to have purely causal antecedents. As noted earlier, the great insight of Davidson was that this dichotomy was a false one, and that action at least could be subsumed under the heading of causal explanation.

In another recent philosophical tradition, represented by Strawson, the problem of agency is really a problem about, for lack of a better word, naturalization. Our practices of moral responsibility appear to conflict with the scientific image of the world, and previous attempts at reconciling these—of being an optimist, in Strawson's terms (Strawson, 1962)— are much too simple. Strawson proposes to carry out the reconciliation

---

[19] This program is not unique to Davidson. It is vital, for example, to the views of David Lewis, as explained in Lewis (1986a).

Introduction: The Philosophy of Agency **XXV**

by turning to the reactive attitudes and giving a naturalistic account of these attitudes and their demands.

As I noted above, both traditions have tended to focus philosophical attention on action, as opposed to agency. Here I want to make a remark not about the content of these traditions but about their methodology. As opposed to approaching agency on its own terms, these traditions both approach agency in a way that is, on the one hand, generalizing and, on the other, defensive.

Begin with the tendency towards generalization. Davidson and Strawson are each concerned with very general philosophical programs to which agency appears to be an exception. Their philosophical strategies are ones of subsumption, of showing how agency can be subsumed under the general heading of the causal, as in Davidson, or of the natural, as in Strawson. Success in these enterprises lies in assimilation, in showing how agency is not so unlike non-agency as it seems to be.

The tendency towards defensiveness has a similar impetus. The dis-analogies between agency and other aspects of the world are presented, often, as arguments: as an argument that a causal account of the world is incomplete, or that our judgments of moral responsibility must be given up. The central goal of philosophical accounts of agency, then, is to answer these arguments, and to show that agency is not as problematic as it seems, after all.

I highlight these methodological tendencies because, like the focus on action as opposed to agency, they color so much recent work in the philosophy of agency. Consider the much-neglected issue of agentive modality.[20] Perhaps the signal achievement in the formally oriented philosophy of the last fifty years has been the articulation of a clear and rigorous semantics—both for logic and for natural language—for modal expressions. This is the 'possible worlds semantics' developed and deployed by a generation of logicians, philosophers, and linguists. Yet, for all its power and breadth, possible worlds semantics is curiously silent on the kind of modality that appears characteristic of agency.

---

[20] While it has indeed gone neglected among philosophers for a long time, there has been a recent resurgence of interest in this vital topic. See, for instance, Maier (2015), Mandelkern et al. (2017), and Willer (2021).

xxvi Introduction: The Philosophy of Agency

The neglect is both formal and substantive. Formally, in the logical tradition from which possible worlds semantics emerges, possibility and necessity are understood as operators on propositions. As we have already said, propositions do not play as central a role in the theory of agency as they do in accounts of language and thought. There is the substantive issue that the distinctive problems that arise in accounts of agency are simply not considered in the development of possible worlds semantics and are dealt with only in later developments.[21]

When agentive modality is considered, it is treated as a special case of the theory of modality generally. This is a manifestation of the generalizing and defensive tendencies in the treatment of agency in recent philosophy. Thus, for instance, Angelika Kratzer (Kratzer, 1981) gives an account of expressions of agentive modality on which they can be understood as a special case of expressions of agentive modality generally. In metaphysics the situation is scarcely better, and we arrive at a general theory of the metaphysics of modality, such as the theory developed in Lewis (1986b), with little to no consideration of agentive issues. Only in more recent years have philosophers of modality begun to feel the strain in this edifice.

In Chap. 2, I will explain why precisely the framework of possible worlds semantics fails to capture agentive modality. Here I simply want to register a methodological point. The project of understanding agentive modality, in recent anglophone philosophy, has gone by way of giving a general theory of modality and then attempting to apply it to the agentive case. This methodology is so entrenched that it can be challenging to conceive of an alternative.

But there is an alternative, which is simply to begin with agency and the modal locutions that are distinctive to it: 'can,' 'is able to,' 'has the ability to,' and others. One can then give an account of agentive modality on its own terms, an account that looks altogether different from the one arrived at from beginning with modality generally. This is the approach one takes when one begins with the philosophy of agency. Indeed, it simply is a part of the philosophy of agency, properly understood.

---

[21] One notable such development is stit logic (Belnap, 1991).

By the lights of recent philosophy this kind of approach to agentive modality can seem idiosyncratic. Yet historically it is a common one. I have already emphasized the discussion of modality in Sartre and in the phenomenological tradition more broadly, where agency plays a central role. This is also the approach taken in a foundational text in the philosophy of modality: Book Theta of Aristotle's *Metaphysics* (Makin, 2006). There Aristotle approaches the topic of possibility not through the topic of propositions but primarily through the abilities of agents. Indeed, whereas the influence of Aristotle on Davidson's philosophy of action has been well-noted, not least by Davidson himself,[22] the full scope of Aristotelian thinking about agency and modality is not so often recalled, as it stands from some remove from the ways of thinking about these topics induced by the possible worlds approach to modality.

This agency-centric approach to modality also closely tracks the developmental psychology of modality. There is considerable evidence that children master expressions having to do with agents before they do the varieties of modality that are more closely tied to propositions, such as epistemic modality.[23] This too is unsurprising: our initial encounter with possibility and necessity is of practical availability and impediment, whereas the structured possibilities involved in thought and talk become salient only later in our dealings with the world.

In short, recent work on modality has exhibited a tendency found in recent philosophical work generally. Agentive notions are treated as a special case, to be handled relatively late in the account. This is directly opposed to both historical tendencies in philosophy as well as to the natural history of modal language. The present approach, on which we begin with the agentive, is intended to restore a more traditional order of inquiry.

This approach parallels the more general methodological theme sounded in the foregoing. Recent work in the philosophy of agency has tended to focus narrowly on the topic of action, at the expense of all the other aspects of agency. Attention to agentive modality—which is just as

---

[22] In Davidson (1980, Essay 1), Davidson clearly emphasizes the indebtedness of his own conception of action explanation to Aristotle's.

[23] For a clear summary of this data, its various interpretations and its bearings on semantic theories of modality, see Papafragou (1998).

central to the philosophy of agency as it is to the philosophy of modality—serves to extend the philosophical gaze to the issue of agency quite generally, to what is possible for agents as well as to what they actually do.

Ultimately, however, these questions of philosophical methodology are not the most central ones. What motivates the wide ambit of the present approach is not merely that recaptures the historical spirit of the philosophy of agency, or that it sets itself problems that the philosophy of action, narrowly conceived, does not even notice—although it does do both of those things. What motivates it ultimately is considerations sounded at the outset. When we think about our own lives and what matters to us, our inactions and our possibilities figure centrally. The philosophy of agency needs to be mindful of absences because any given agent's life is constituted by what that agent does not do, as well as what she does. Agency, from without but most of all from within, is characterized by inaction, regret, and possibilities foregone.[24] It is also, however, also inevitably directed forward, towards options available and things to be done. This divided consciousness is an inescapable aspect of being an agent, and the philosophy of agency should aim, at least, at making it better understood.

Bibliography

Belnap, N. (1991). Backwards and Forwards in the Modal Logic of Agency. *Philosophy and Phenomenological Research, 51*(4), 777–807.
Bratman, M. (1987). *Intention, Plans, and Practical Reason.* Harvard University Press.
Chalmers, D. J. (1996). *The Conscious Mind: In Search of a Fundamental Theory.* Oxford University Press.
Clarke, R. (2014). *Omissions: Agency, Metaphysics, and Responsibility.* Oxford University Press.

---

[24] It is this essentially shadowed aspect of the human experience that William James has in mind when he writes: *Take the happiest man, the one most envied by the world, and in nine cases out of ten his inmost consciousness is one of failure. Either his ideals in the line of his achievements are pitched far higher than the achievements themselves, or else he has secret ideals of which the world knows nothing, and in regard to which he inwardly knows himself to be found wanting* (James, 1902, p. 137).

Davidson, D. (1980). *Essays on Actions and Events*. Oxford University Press.

Davidson, D. (1980, Essay 1). Actions, Reasons, and Causes. In (Davidson, 1980).

Davidson, D. (1980, Essay 3). Agency. In (Davidson, 1980).

Davidson, D. (1980, Essay 4). Freedom to Act. In (Davidson, 1980).

Davidson, D. (1984). *Inquiries into Truth and Interpretation*. Oxford University Press.

Fischer, J. M., & Ravizza, M. (1998). *Responsibility and Control: A Theory of Moral Responsibility*. Cambridge University Press.

Frankfurt, H. G. (1969). Alternate Possibilities and Moral Responsibility. *The Journal of Philosophy, 66*(23), 829–839.

Hampshire, S. (1959). *Thought and Action*. Chatto & Windus.

James, W. (1902). *The Varieties of Religious Experience: A Study in Human Nature*. Longmans Green.

Kratzer, A. (1981). The Notional Category of Modality. In H. J. Eikmeyer & H. Rieser (Eds.), *Words, Worlds, and Contexts*. De Gruyter.

Lewis, D. K. (1986a). Causal Explanation. In *Philosophical Papers Vol. II*. Oxford University Press.

Lewis, D. K. (1986b). *On the Plurality of Worlds*. Wiley-Blackwell

Maier, J. (2014). The Argument from Moral Responsibility. *Australasian Journal of Philosophy, 92*(2), 249–267

Maier, J. (2015). The Agentive Modalities. *Philosophy and Phenomenological Research, 90*(1), 113–134.

Maier, J. (2020). Abilities. In *The Stanford Encyclopedia of Philosophy* (E.N. Zalta, Ed.). Metaphysics Research Lab, Stanford University.

Makin, S. (2006). *Aristotle: Metaphysics Theta*. Oxford University Press.

Mandelkern, M., Schultheis, G., & Boylan, D. (2017). Agentive Modals. *Philosophical Review, 126*(3), 301–343.

O'Hara, J. (1934). *Appointment in Samarra*. Harcourt Brace.

Papafragou, A. (1998). The Acquisition of Modality: Implications for Theories of Semantic Representation. *Mind and Language, 13*(3), 370–399.

Sartre, J. P. (1956). *Being and Nothingness: An Essay on Phenomenological Ontology* (H. E. Barnes, trans.). Routledge.

Stanley, J., & Williamson, T. (2001). Knowing How. *Journal of Philosophy, 98*(8), 411–444.

Steward, H. (2012). *A Metaphysics for Freedom*. Oxford University Press.

Strawson, G. (1994). The Impossibility of Moral Responsibility. *Philosophical Studies, 75*(1/2), 5–24.

Strawson, P. F. (1962). Freedom and Resentment. *Proceedings of the British Academy, 48*, 1–25.

Thompson, M. (2008). *Life and Action: Elementary Structures of Practice and Practical Thought.* Harvard University Press.

van Inwagen, P. (1989). When is the Will Free? *Philosophical Perspectives, 3*, 399–422.

Velleman, J. D. (1989). Epistemic Freedom. *Pacific Philosophical Quarterly, 70*(1), 73–97.

Velleman, J. D. (1992). What Happens When Someone Acts? *Mind, 101*(403), 461–481.

Wallace, R. J. (2013). *The View from Here: On Affirmation, Attachment, and the Limits of Regret.* Oxford University Press.

Willer, M. (2021). Two Puzzles About Ability Can. *Linguistics and Philosophy, 44*(3), 551–586.

1

Foundations

1.1 Options Introduced

This book addresses certain foundational questions in the philosophy of agency: the relationship between agency and possibility, the nature of ability, and the conflict between the freedom of agents and the governance of natural law. These are questions that have occupied philosophers since antiquity, and they are ones to which the present account gives a response that is comprehensive, unified, and, I argue, correct.

This response will take some time to develop, but its basic idea is simple. To be an agent to is to be a being with options: acts that are available to be performed. For any agent, at any time, there are many acts that are options for that agent—and there are many acts that are *not* options for that agent.

Furthermore, there is no reductive analysis of what it is for an agent to have an act as an option. Options are not to be analyzed in terms of conditionals, or in terms of other allegedly more basic varieties of possibility. For an agent, options are fundamental.

This idea—agents have options, and that there is no reductive analysis of what it is to have an option—is not a new one, and indeed in certain

© The Author(s), under exclusive license to Springer Nature Switzerland AG 2022
J. T. Maier, *Options and Agency*, https://doi.org/10.1007/978-3-031-10243-1_1

moods it can seem almost platitudinous. If it already seems clear and unobjectionable, then so much to the better. This is not a book that debates a speculative hypothesis but one that stubbornly pursues the implications of a simple and recalcitrant fact.

Many of these implications are broadly constructive ones. The foregoing has emphasized the resistance of options to philosophical analysis, and that theme will be developed and elaborated in what follows. But though options are not fit to be an analysandum, they are well-fitted to be an analysans. Once options are admitted as fundamental, otherwise opaque phenomena may be explained and made clear in terms of options.

So, while the project proposed here begins in insisting on the fundamentality of a certain notion, it does not end there. It insists on explaining much else in terms of the fundamental notion of an option. In fact, those explanations give us reason to believe that we were right to take options as fundamental in the first place. It is precisely in virtue of their simplicity and clarity that careful attention to options can illuminate the entire practical realm.

1.2 Options and Possibility

When we describe an agent considering what to do, there are several modes of expression available to us. We may speak of what the agent *can* do, what she *is able to* do, what acts are *possible for her*, what acts are *available to her*, or what acts *are in her power*. Underneath this linguistic diversity, I propose, is a metaphysical unity. These are ways of describing her *options*.

Options, so demarcated, appear to be intimately connected to possibility. Indeed, at least one of the locutions just listed—'possible for'—explicitly appeals to possibility. And linguists have proposed semantics for several of the other expressions in our list in terms of quantification over possible worlds. And these linguistic considerations are supported by our own informal reflections on options. When I say that someone has raising her arm as an option, I appear to be somehow invoking a certain

1 Foundations   3

possible situation, one in which she raises her arm.[1] So if we want to give a general account of options, it is tempting to immediately prescind from the niceties of options and concern ourselves directly with possibility.

We should not be too quick, however, to assimilate options to possibility generally, for at least two reasons.

First, there is a natural distinction to be drawn between the various eventualities that might befall an agent, on the one hand, and the various things that she can do, on the other. An agent might be at some risk of falling into a swimming pool (due to the uneven footing at the edges), and also may be at some risk of jumping into that same swimming pool (due to her spontaneous nature).[2] Both of these mark possibilities for an agent, but only the latter of them marks one of her options. The category of possibility is too coarse-grained to figure in an informal characterization of what options are, as it lumps together distinctions that ought to be kept distinct.

---

[1] This possible situation is not a 'possible world' in the ordinary sense of that term. For one thing, possible worlds are global and comprehensive, whereas the situations invoked by claims about options are local and partial. Further asymmetries between options and the framework of possible worlds will be canvassed in what follows.

[2] Here it is instructive to consider Sartre's discussion of vertigo: *I am on a narrow path-without a guard-rail-which goes along a precipice. The precipice presents itself to me as to be avoided; it represents a danger of death. At the same time I conceive of a certain number of causes, originating in universal determinism, which can transform that threat of death into reality; I can slip on a stone and fall into the abyss; the crumbling earth of the path can give way under my steps. Through these various anticipations, I am given to myself as a thing; I am passive in relation to these possibilities; they come to me from without; in so far as I am also an object in the world, subject to gravitation, they are my possibilities. At this moment fear appears, which in terms of the situation is the apprehension of myself as a destructible transcendent in the midst of transcendents, as an object which does not contain in itself the origin of its future disappearance. My reaction will be of the reflective order; I will pay attention to the stones in the road; I will keep myself as far as possible from the edge of the path. I realize myself as pushing away the threatening situation with all my strength, and I project before myself a certain number of future conducts destined to keep the threats of the world at a distance from me. These conducts are my possibilities* (Sartre, 1956, p. 30).

Sartre, as I understand him, is drawing a distinction between two kinds of possibilities: the possibilities with respect to which I am passive, and the possibilities with respect to which I am active—my 'conducts.' A generic notion of possibility lumps together these two varieties of possibility. The notion of an option, in contrast, marks this distinction clearly: it is just when I 'project before myself a certain number of future conducts destined to keep the threats of the world at a distance from me' that I address myself to my options, rather than to the 'various anticipations' that come to me 'in so far as I am also an object in the world.' Options, we might say, arise only for beings who exist *pour soi*.

It may of course be that options may yet be modeled as a species of possibility, in a way that could accommodate this and other distinctions. This has indeed been the tendency in formal thinking about possibility. We elaborate a general framework for modeling possibility—the framework of possible worlds—and then model the varieties of possibility within that very general framework, as special cases. If this could be done, then we could indeed treat options as one kind of possibility.

I will eventually argue that this project fails, and this is the second reason for resisting this possibilist line of thought in our thinking about options. Options are intimately connected to possibility, that connection is a subtle one, which runs in one direction only: claims about options entail claims about possibility, but the converse is not in general true. Options may not therefore be analyzed in terms of possibility, nor can they be modeled in terms of the framework of possible worlds.

That argument will be given in the next chapter. Here it suffices to emphasize that we should not assume, at the outset, that options are a species of possibility. They will need to be understood on their own terms.

1.3 Options and Choice Situations

Options are described by a verbal motley of expressions. They are not to be assimilated to another metaphysical category, such as the category of possibility. How then do we arrive at a clear conception of what options are?

The best way to appreciate what options are is not by using certain expressions, or by availing ourselves of formal frameworks, but by considering what is true in a certain case. A simple case will do. Imagine someone is in a store, with five dollars in her pocket. A newspaper costs one dollar, a pen costs two dollars, and a notebook costs four dollars. This is a *choice situation.*

Options are to be understood in terms of their role in choice situations. The agent just described, for example, has several options. For example, she has buying only a pen as an option, and she has buying a notebook and a newspaper as an option. At the same time, there are several acts that are not options for her. For example, she does not have the option of buying a notebook and a pen.

This brief description suffices to indicate the significance of options. If we want to give this person advice about what to do, or explain what she does, and perhaps to blame or praise her for what she does, then the first thing we want to know is what her options are. The significance of options will be discussed and further elaborated in the next section.

This description also allows us to think more rigorously about the logic of options. For example, this principle indicates that an agent's options are not in general preserved when conjoined with other options. From the fact that an agent has some act as an option, and some other act as an option, it does not follow that she has the conjunction of these acts as an option. This does not follow because, while the agent described above has both buying a pen and buying a notebook as an option, she does not have buying a pen and a notebook as an option. So we can begin to systematize our judgments about options by seeing what principles are, and are not, valid in the logic of options.

Finally, in addition to showing what options are, this example shows, just as importantly, what they are not.

Options are not to be identified with simple or basic acts. On certain philosophical views, there are basic acts, acts which we do without doing anything else. And, on certain philosophical views, our only options are, in fact, basic acts. But these are substantive views about agency, rather than definitional views about options. As a formal matter, our options may be any act whatsoever: raising one's arm may be an option for an agent, but so too may a more complex act, such as buying a pen.

Relatedly, an agents' options will depend not only on how she herself is, but also on her environment. Whether an agent has buying a pen as an option will depend partly on her psychological and physical makeup, but it will depend also on a host of factors that are external to her and over which she has no immediate control: the presence of a store, that market having pens in stock, indeed the very existence and stability of the currency system. The question of whether an agent has an act as an option will typically depend on more than the agent herself, and at times may encompass broad states of the world in which she finds herself.

Options are basic in the theory of agency. But they are not basic in the sense of being atomic, in the way that basic acts are sometimes supposed to be. Rather, I will argue, they are basic in the sense of being primitive from the point of view of analysis and explanation. There is nothing more fundamental than options in terms of which options can be analyzed or explained.

1.4 Knowledge of Options

These metaphysical observations about options have an immediate epistemic corollary. If our options were atomic acts that did not depend in any way on our environment, then perhaps we would always be in a position to know what our options are.[3] But our options are typically not like this. My options will be complex acts that depend on the environment in ways that I cannot always ascertain. The question of whether I have the option of buying a newspaper at a store will depend, in part, on whether that shop has newspapers in stock, and this is something that I may be ignorant about. Therefore, I may be ignorant of whether I have the option of buying a newspaper at that store.

This then marks another way in which options are not basic. As they are not atomic, so are they not certain. An agent can be wrong, and often is wrong, about what her options are. There is in general no necessary connection between an agent's options on the one hand and her beliefs or knowledge about her options on the other.

This simple point is liable to be neglected, for several reasons.

The first is that we typically disregard the options of which an agent is simply unaware. If a certain code will unlock a safe, and I have the option of entering that code into the safe, then I have the option of opening the safe. We will often ignore this option for the purposes of evaluation and advice, but it is there nonetheless. I propose to focus on the unrestricted notion of an option, and to understand more epistemically restricted notions in terms of it. Davidson writes that there is a sense of 'can' on

---

[3] See however Williamson (2000) for a far-reaching argument that even purportedly local and simple conditions—such as being in pain—are not transparent to us.

which 'every one of us could make a million dollars on the stock market, marry a movie star, or even bring an end to the war. If only we knew how' (Davidson, 1980, Essay 4, p. 66). It is this broad and unrestricted sense of what courses of action are open to us (if only we knew) that corresponds to the notion of an option.

Another reason is more theoretical. There has been a sustained interest in recent philosophy in the nature of practical knowledge, and the many ways in which an agent's actions are guided by what she knows. This epistemic orientation is welcome, but it can sometimes obscure the respects in which action is almost a domain in which ignorance looms large. As we have come to accept that our own minds are often opaque and inaccessible to us, so too should we accept that the range of acts that are available to us may be something we apprehend, at best, imperfectly. To be an agent is to be a being with options, but not always to know precisely what those options are.

The last reason is also a theoretical one. Options appear to figure prominently in contemporary formal frameworks for understanding how agents do, and should, make choices under conditions of uncertainty—a set of frameworks collectively known as 'decision theory.' Thus, for instance, a recent introduction to decision theory writes: 'for agents to face a genuine decision problem they must have options: actions that they are capable of performing and equally of foregoing if they so choose' (Bradley, 2018). Options, as they figure in decision theory, are transparent to the agent whose options they are (Schwarz, 2021). This may lead to the impression that options, as they figure here, are transparent as well.

But options as they figure in decision theory are, as I understand it, simply an idealization of our working notion of an option. And one of the ways in which decision theory idealizes away from our actual situation is by supposing that our options are transparent to us. But they are not actually so. We should not too closely conflate the present notion of an option with options as they figure in decision theory, although the two notions are indeed cognates and aptly described by the same term.

1.5 Why Options Matter

There are several reasons why an agent's options matter, both to the agent herself and anyone who wishes to explain or evaluate her behavior.

The first has already been given. Options are essential to articulating a basic fact about agents about ourselves, namely that we are often—indeed, almost always—in a choice situation. That is, we face several possible acts, between which we can deliberate and among which we might choose. These 'possible acts' are simply an agent's options, and in this sense our very predicament cannot even be described without appeal to options.[4]

A second reason why options matter is that they are integral to our evaluations of our own lives, and those of others, as going well or poorly. An unhappy life in which many options for happiness were missed might seem more lamentable, on balance, than an equally unhappy one in which there were no such options. This option-sensitivity of our evaluation of lives is especially marked in the sentiment of regret: regret takes as its object, in the typical case, an act that one had as an option but that one failed to perform.[5]

A third reason why options matter is that they are sometimes held to be salient to judgments about moral responsibility. Several writers have suggested, for example, that an agent is blameworthy for an act only if she had the option of performing some other act instead.[6] Options, more generally, have been thought to be central to our practices of blame, resentment, and exculpation.

We have, therefore, several reasons for holding that options matter. All three of these reasons involve how things that matter to us—deliberation, evaluation, and moral responsibility—depend on options, and in this

---

[4] Enoch (2013) makes the intriguing proposal that certain objects are deliberatively indispensable, in parallel to the traditional notion of explanatory indispensability. The considerations outlined here suggest that options are, in this sense, deliberatively indispensable.

[5] Work in psychology suggests that the most common objects of regret are opportunities that one did not pursue, especially educational opportunities (Roese & Summerville, 2005).

[6] This is a formulation, in terms of options, of Harry Frankfurt's 'principle of alternate possibilities' (PAP) discussed in the Introduction, according to which 'a person is morally responsible for what he has done only if he could have done otherwise' (Frankfurt, 1969).

sense the importance of options is derivative. In the remainder of the discussion, I will show that options also have an independent and theoretical significance: they figure as constructive elements in the theory of agency. Taken together, these two sets of considerations tell in favor of giving options a central place in the account of deliberative agents like ourselves.

1.6 Options and Free Will

Given their significance, it is surprising that options are not more frequently discussed. If one considers the redoubtable problems of contemporary philosophy, one encounters talk of knowledge, of normativity, of consciousness—but seldom does one encounter much explicit talk about options.

Partly this is due to terminology. Earlier I mentioned the variety of phrases in English that can be used to pick out an agent's options. This linguistic diversity is a part, also, of philosophical language. In decision theory, for example, options are called by various alternative names, such as 'prospects.' There is not a single settled name for what I am talking about, which can lead to the false impression that options are less prominent in philosophical discussions than they are.

Beyond this terminological consideration, however, it is true that options are relatively neglected in many contemporary philosophical discussions. The most significant reason for this is connected, I believe, to a nexus of issues surrounding what has come to be called 'the problem of free will.'

There are in fact several problems that go under the heading of 'free will,' but one has taken on special prominence in recent philosophy. This is the problem of reconciling our claims about moral responsibility with the fact that our world is, or might be, deterministic. In particular, the following argument has been central to this discussion:

10   J. T. Maier

(P1) Determinism is (or might be) true
(P2) If determinism is true, then agents do not have options[7]
(P3) If agents do not have options, then they are not morally responsible for what they do
(C) Agents are not (or might not be) morally responsible for what they do

This argument has loomed large in previous discussions of options. Let us consider it in some detail.

The first premise, P1, is simply a plausible claim about the world. Determinism is an empirical hypothesis that may or may not be true. Our best theories about the world are quantum mechanical, but quantum mechanics admits of a deterministic interpretation.[8] P1 is simply a plausible claim about the physics of our world, and the fact that our knowledge of final physics remains incomplete.[9]

The second premise, P2, poses a profound challenge to the vision of agency and the world articulated here. It indicates a conflict between options—which I have argued are thoroughly intertwined with our practical lives—and the live physical hypothesis of determinism. The most powerful argument for P2 is an argument known as the Consequence

---

[7] There is an important qualification here. As traditionally understood, determinism does not threaten the very possibility of action (though see Steward (2012)). It simply threatens the possibility of being able to act otherwise than one in fact does. In the next chapter, I will argue for what I will call the Performance Principle: if an agent performs an act, then she has that act has an option. So, according to most philosophers, agents act in a deterministic world, and therefore have some options—namely, the option of doing whatever they actually do. Therefore, there is a reading of P2 on which most philosophers will hold it is straightforwardly false, so long as agents act in a deterministic world.

I have in mind a more demanding reading of 'options' in P2. On this reading, 'options' refers to the options that agents have to perform acts that they do not actually perform. This is a natural reading of the term, although not the only one. When we consider these arguments at length in Chap. 7, I will introduce the phrase 'unexercised options' to explicitly refer to those acts that an agent has as options but does not perform. In these terms, a more accurate and explicit formulation of P2 would be: 'If determinism is true, then agents do not have unexercised options.' For now that qualification will be left implicit.

[8] There is good evidence that quantum mechanics is actually true of our world, but that does not necessarily tell against P1, for there are deterministic interpretations of quantum mechanics (Goldstein, 2021).

[9] It bears emphasizing that P1 concerns the epistemic, rather than the metaphysical, possibility of determinism—it concerns the fact that, for all we know, our world might be deterministic. As I will argue in Chap. 6, there are good reasons for thinking that it is the epistemic possibility of determinism that is at issue in the free will debates.

1 Foundations 11

Argument. Understanding the Consequence Argument, and the considerations in favor of P2, will be one of the central tasks of the discussion to follow.

The third premise, P3, echoes one of the reasons why options matter given in the previous section. Options, many authors have held, are a necessary condition on morally responsible agency. Therefore, any threat to options from determinism—as P1 and P2 suggest—is a threat to moral responsibility itself.

A prominent response to this argument in recent philosophy has proceeded as follows. Both premises P1 and P2 are taken to be compelling. This response, therefore, grants them. Nonetheless, it is argued, premise P3 is false. There are a couple of ways in which this might be argued.

The first is to suggest that the grounds of moral responsibility lie ultimately in the reactive attitudes, such as resentment, that these may be upheld in a deterministic world, and therefore that the practices of moral responsibility that they ground may be upheld as well. This approach to moral responsibility is suggested by a pathbreaking essay by P.F. Strawson (Strawson, 1962) and has been developed in a sustained way by R. Jay Wallace (Wallace, 1994), among others.

The second approach considers our judgments about certain cases. Consider the premise P3, or a particular implementation of that principle: an agent is morally responsible for some act A only if she has the option of performing some distinct act B instead. This principle captures the intuitive thought that one is not morally responsible for what one is compelled to do.[10] Harry Frankfurt, however, asks us to reflect on the following sort of case (Frankfurt, 1969). A person commits some crime: she steals some money. A neuroscientist had been monitoring her brain activity: if she had tried to decide not to steal the money, he would have intervened so that she would have decided to steal the money after all. As it happens, she decided to steal the money on her own, so the neuroscientist did not need to intervene. There was no act B such that she had the option of doing B instead of A. Her only option was to do A. Nonetheless, she is morally responsible for doing A. So our principle is false. Cases like

---

[10] This is, once again, Frankfurt's 'principle of alternate possibilities'—a principle that, for reasons to be discussed presently, Frankfurt holds that we should reject.

these have led authors to develop accounts of moral responsibility on which options are not a condition on moral responsibility, the most developed of which is perhaps (Fischer & Ravizza, 1998).

These distinct but related challenges to P3 are, I believe, deeply compelling. While I believe the final word on these issues has yet to be written, the insight that moral responsibility and options are not as tightly bound to each other as we once took them to be is a major step forward in our understanding of moral responsibility.[11] The ongoing project of working out the conditions of moral responsibility, in light of these considerations, is I believe among the most important research programs in contemporary moral philosophy.

The following, however, needs to be emphasized: options matter *even if* options are altogether irrelevant to moral responsibility. Indeed, *most* of the case for the significance of options goes through even if options are altogether irrelevant to moral responsibility. If agents do not have options, then our conceptions of ourselves as deliberative agents is fundamentally mistaken, decision theory as traditionally conceived does not apply to us, and our standards of evaluating our own lives are misguided. If determinism is true and the Consequence Argument is sound, then we are in these ways in error about our predicament. Thus, whatever the truth about moral responsibility, any challenge to options is a profound challenge to our conception of ourselves.

I emphasize these points because they are not always, I believe, acknowledged. Much of the literature gives the impression that, so long as moral responsibility is secured, the conclusion that agents do not have

---

[11] While P3 is probably too simple a principle, the arguments against it do not seem to me to indicate that options are never required for moral responsibility. In particular, options seem to be involved in our judgments about moral responsibility for omissions. As noted in the Introduction, omissions are central to the philosophy of agency, but have not always been treated as such. Nonetheless, for present purposes, I will argue that options are crucial even if we hold the extreme position that they never figure among the conditions of moral responsibility.

1 Foundations   13

options may be reasonably accepted.[12] But this is just a mistake: if agents do not (or might not) have options, then drastically revisionary consequences follow.

It is the neglect of these observations that, I believe, has led to the neglect of options. These are relatively elementary points, so it may be surprising that they are not recognized more frequently. One culprit may be the phrase 'free will.' As noted above, on one understanding of that phrase, it refers narrowly to the conditions on moral responsibility. On that understanding, then, on at least some of the accounts of moral responsibility offered above, it may be that agents have free will even if they do not have options, and that determinism is no threat to free will even if the Consequence Argument is sound.

That is a perfectly legitimate use of the term, but I want to emphasize that there is also another, broader, use. On this use, an agent has free will just in case she has options. On this construal, moral responsibility may be one upshot of free will, but it is only one. Free will applies broadly to our practical lives, independently of specifically moral considerations of blame and praise. I believe contemporary discussions have tended to

---

[12] One statement of this view is suggested in the following remark from Frank Jackson: 'Even the most dedicated compatibilists identify [the Consequence Argument] as the argument they need to rebut. What compatibilist arguments show, or so it seems to me, is not that free action as understood by the folk is compatible with determinism, but that free action on a conception near enough to the folk's to be regarded as a natural extension of it, and which does the theoretical job we folk give the concept of free action in adjudicating questions of moral responsibility and punishment ... is compatible with determinism.' (Jackson, 1998, pp. 44–45).

One way of understanding this rich remark is that we might give up options to the Consequence Argument and yet retain whatever is needed of free action to adjudicate questions of moral responsibility. We might, as it were, get by with free action *modulo* options. The view taken here is that this strategy, if indeed it is what Jackson has in mind, is not really a feasible one at all, for so much else depends on options.

1.7 Plan of the Book

The remainder of this book, then, is concerned with understanding options, and then with understanding other phenomena in terms of options, and finally with addressing the free will disputes from the point of view of a clear understanding of options.

The next chapter, Chap. 2, is concerned with defending a central thesis of this book: there is no reductive analysis of what it is to have an option. Options are analytically primitive. I argue that there are problems for standard approaches to analyzing options, and that these turn on fundamental aspects of our practical lives. While options are primitive, we can nonetheless say quite a lot about them, about both their metaphysics and the logical principles that govern them, and I aim to say just that in the course of this chapter.

Chapter 3 turns to putting options to work and explaining other practical phenomena in terms of options. Since Aristotle, philosophers have been concerned to give an account of ability. I argue that, once we have a clear appreciation of options, we can give such an account. We can at the same time give an account of the semantics of ability ascriptions in natural language. Finally, in terms of abilities, we can give an account of skills, talents, and other such phenomena. The construction that emerges is a unified account of agentive modality on which agents' options figure as the keystone.

---

[13] This is, I believe, a distinctively contemporary tendency. If one consults earlier discussions of free will, moral responsibility does not loom nearly as large. To take one example, John Bramhall offers a number of arguments for 'liberty' in his dispute with Hobbes (Hobbes & Bramhall, 1999): these include the fact that agents are able to choose to choose to follow God, that agents are able to refrain (as opposed to merely omitting to act), and that we are the subject of commands that we may nonetheless disobey. The issue of moral responsibility enters only indirectly, and, even then, in admixture with other, typically theological, considerations: *A man can never make himself a criminal if he be not left at liberty to commit a crime ... To take away liberty hazards heaven, but undoubtedly it leaves no hell* (Hobbes & Bramhall, 1999, p. 4). The focus on principles such as P3 in contemporary discussions would have been alien both to Bramhall and to Hobbes.

Chapter 4 turns from agentive powers specifically to the theory of powers generally. A number of recent philosophers have defended the idea that agents' abilities are to be analyzed in terms of dispositions. Chapter 4 develops an account on which has things the wrong way around. The dispositions of objects are passive powers to be acted on in certain ways by agents. It is the active powers of agents, which in turn are to be understood in terms of options, which constitute the foundation for a general theory of powers.

Chapter 5 steps back and considers the picture of agentive possibility that emerges from the foregoing discussion. It is a picture that is different both from the 'Humean' approaches that have predominated in much contemporary philosophy of mind and action and from the 'Aristotelian' approaches that have been proposed as an alternative. The view of agentive possibility defended here, which resists reductive proposals but also resists the reification of agentive powers, fits neatly into neither one of these categories.

These five chapters are constructive: I say what options are (Chap. 1), argue that they are primitive (Chap. 2), given an account of abilities in terms of options (Chap. 3), give an account of powers generally in terms of abilities (Chap. 4), and finally sketch the picture of agentive possibility that emerges from these metaphysical and semantic considerations (Chap. 5).

Chapter 6, in contrast, is critical. I consider the program of responding to the Consequence Argument by giving an account of agency that either (1) gives an analysis of options or (2) does not appeal to options at all. I argue that this program may satisfy certain purposes, such as giving an account of the conditions on moral responsibility, but it fails to give an adequate account of what it is to be an agent. If we are to defend compatibilism, conciliatory attempts to reduce options or to do without options altogether are not the approach that we should take.

Finally, in Chap. 7 I defend a response to the free will question more consonant with the view defended in the foregoing, a view that I call *simple compatibilism*. The proper way of responding to the Consequence Argument is precisely by resisting sophisticated strategies of reconciliation and taking options to be a simple and irreducible feature of the world, at the same level of fundamentality as the laws themselves. The Consequence Argument inevitably relies on a substantive principle linking options and laws. It is that principle that the simple compatibilist rejects. The resultant view is distinct from both sophisticated compatibilism on the one hand and incompatibilism on the other. It represents a position that breaks with the increasing levels of dialectical and analytical subtlety that characterize the contemporary free will disputes, and which allows for compatibilism to rest on a simple yet comprehensive account of the very foundations of agency.

Bibliography

Bradley, R. (2018). Decision Theory: A Formal Theoretical Introduction. In *Introduction to Formal Philosophy* (pp. 611–655). Springer.

Davidson, D. (1980). *Essays on Actions and Events*. Oxford University Press.

Davidson, D. (1980, Essay 4). Freedom to Act. In (Davidson, 1980).

Enoch, D. (2013). *Taking Morality Seriously: A Defense of Robust Realism*. Oxford University Press.

Fischer, J. M., & Ravizza, M. (1998). *Responsibility and Control: A Theory of Moral Responsibility*. Cambridge University Press.

Frankfurt, H. G. (1969). Alternate Possibilities and Moral Responsibility. *The Journal of Philosophy, 66*(23), 829–839.

Goldstein, S. (2021). Bohmian Mechanics. In E. N. Zalta (Ed.), *The Stanford Encyclopedia of Philosophy*. Metaphysics Research Lab, Stanford University.

Hobbes, T., & Bramhall, J. (1999). *Hobbes and Bramhall on Liberty and Necessity* (V. Chappell, ed.). Cambridge University Press.

Jackson, F. (1998). *From Metaphysics to Ethics: A Defence of Conceptual Analysis*. Oxford University Press.

Roese, N. J., & Summerville, A. (2005). What We Regret Most … and Why. *Personality and Social Psychology Bulletin, 31*(9), 1273–1285.

Sartre, J. P. (1956). *Being and Nothingness: An Essay on Phenomenological Ontology* (H. E. Barnes, trans.). Routledge.

Schwarz, W. (2021). Objects of Choice. *Mind, 130*(517), 165–197.

Steward, H. (2012). *A Metaphysics for Freedom*. Oxford University Press.

Strawson, P. F. (1962). Freedom and Resentment. *Proceedings of the British Academy, 48*, 1–25.

Wallace, R. J. (1994). *Responsibility and the Moral Sentiments*. Harvard University Press.

Williamson, T. (2000). *Knowledge and Its Limits*. Oxford University Press.

2

The Simplicity of Options

2.1 Having Options

On the view to be defended here, agents have certain acts as options, and equally do not have certain other acts as options. What is it for an agent to have an act as an option?

On one reading, this question asks for a reductive account of what it is for an agent to have an act as an option in some other terms. I will argue that, in this sense, the question does not have an informative answer. There is no reductive account of what it is for an agent to have an option.

On another reading, this question simply asks for the formal structure of what is involved in having an option, and the principles that govern that structure. In this sense, the question does have an answer. Here I will spell out the formal structure of having an option, and later I will elaborate its governing principles—principles that will, taken together, constitute a logic for options.

Begin with an agent who has an act as an option. For example, a person might have purchasing a newspaper as an option. Here the agent will be that person—Susan, say—and the act will be the act of purchasing a newspaper. As I will understand it, for an agent to have an act as an

---

© The Author(s), under exclusive license to Springer Nature Switzerland AG 2022
J. T. Maier, *Options and Agency*, https://doi.org/10.1007/978-3-031-10243-1_2

option is for a certain relation to hold. This is the option relation, a dyadic relation which takes an agent and an act as its relata:

$$S \text{ OPT } \alpha^1$$

In the example just described, we may take the agent variable 'S' to denote Susan and the act variable a to denote the act of purchasing a newspaper. We can now say, in a more formally perspicuous way, what it is for an agent to have an act as an option. An agent has an act as an option just in case she stands in the option relation to that act.

This relation itself is, I will argue, a basic one. But we may say more about each of its relata.

First, agents. Agents include human beings with typical psychology and physiology, but they need not be restricted to them. For one thing, there are compelling reasons—lately articulated with great force by Helen Steward (Steward, 2012)—for including non-human animals within the scope of the theory of action. In the opposite, or anyhow different, direction, it is important to include non-biological beings, even ones radically different from us, within the scope of the discussion. This includes divine beings, who have been the object of much traditional thinking about agency and freedom. It also includes digital beings, who might have psychologies radically different from our own (Bostrom, 2014) and may, nonetheless, have options.

This catholic construal of agency bears emphasis for two reasons. First, it is yet another reason for detaching questions about options from questions about moral responsibility. Someone may doubt whether even intelligent non-human animals—dolphins, for example—are morally responsible agents, but she may nonetheless grant that they act, and have options. Second, it tells against purported analyses of options that lean heavily on contingent aspects of human psychology. A famous analysis subject to exactly this concern will be considered in the next section.

---

[1] As noted in the previous chapter, 'S' here is a free variable ranging over agents, the Greek letter α is a free variable ranging over acts, and 'OPT' denotes having an option, where this is a relation between an agent and an act.

2 The Simplicity of Options   19

Next, acts. Acts as I will understand them are abstract objects: they may be realized by particular worldly events, but are not to be identified with any such events, or with classes of such events.[2] For an agent to have an act as an option, then, is for her to stand in a relation to a certain abstract object, and to do so in virtue of her actual psychology, physiology, and environment, none of which are themselves abstract. This is in a way puzzling, but no more puzzling than the idea that belief, for instance, involves a relation between an agent and another kind of abstract object, namely a proposition.[3]

What acts exist? At first approximation, there are at least as many acts as there are verb phrases in natural language.[4] Thus there is an act of purchasing a newspaper, of purchasing a newspaper quickly, of purchasing a newspaper for one's friend, and so forth.[5] On the view to be favored here, this is not because acts depend in any sense on language, but because language affords an effective means of describing the acts that are there anyway. In fact, I will later argue for the view that there are many more acts than may be concisely described in natural language.

In short, the view of agents and acts offered here is considerably more copious than that on offer in other recent discussions. There are very many kinds of agents, and very many kinds of acts. Nonetheless, the subsequent discussion addresses structural issues that arise on almost any theory of agency whatsoever, and so it will suffice to focus on relatively uncomplicated and uncontroversial cases of action, those involving a human being bringing about a certain desired outcome, in a relatively circumscribed region of space and in a relatively brief duration of time—for example, buying a newspaper.

---

[2] In the language that predominates in much philosophy of action, acts are 'act-types' rather than 'act-tokens.'

[3] In many ways, I believe, acts play the role in practical reasoning that propositions play in theoretical reasoning. For a sympathetic account of the role of acts as the object of intention, see Baier (1970).

[4] This count is at best approximate, for there are verb phrases that correspond to no act, or nothing an agent does, such as—at least in the typical case—'tripped,' 'fell asleep,' or 'sneezed.'

[5] The view of 'act-individuation' favored here is the kind of fine-grained approach advocated in Goldman (1970).

2.2 The Conditional Analysis

Let us consider the most prominent kind of analysis in the philosophical literature. On this proposal, an agent's options are to be understood in terms of the counterfactual dependence of her acts on her volitions. More specifically:

(CA) S OPT α just in case if S were to choose to α she would α

For example, Susan has the option of purchasing a newspaper just in case she would purchase a newspaper if she chose to.

Before criticizing this analysis, it bears emphasizing its aims. First, while CA is stated in terms of a biconditional, it is ultimately a component of an analysis of options, an account of what it is to have options in other terms. CA connects options to certain counterfactuals, but counterfactuals in turn may be understood in more general terms (perhaps in terms, as suggested by Stalnaker (1968) and Lewis (1973), of quantification over possible worlds). Therefore CA may be regarded as a component of an ambitious research program, of giving an account of agentive modality within a framework for the treatment of modality more generally.

Second, CA as understood is an account of options, and not of anything else. In the next chapter I will consider an array of different agentive modalities, and for all I will argue in this chapter it may be the case—though ultimately, I will argue, it is not the case—that some of these may be analyzed in terms of conditionals. Given the long history of the appeal to conditionals in attempts to account for agency, it may well be that many or most of the conditional analyses considered in the previous literature are not analyses of options in the sense considered here.

So we will be concerned specifically with the conditional analysis of options. Conditional analyses of other agentive notions fall out of the scope of our proposal. So too do analyses of something like options that involve a conditional but that also appeal to some primitive variety of agentive modality (such as Mandelkern et al. (2017)). The target of discussion is, in both these respects, highly specific.

2 The Simplicity of Options 21

When it is construed in this way, how does CA fare? I think it is clear that it fails, and that it fails in ways that reveal certain fundamental obstacles to this kind of proposal more generally. There are at least three different counterexamples to CA.

The first and the simplest counterexample runs as follows. Consider someone who is positioned like the shopper who we have been considering: she has five dollars in her pocket, in a store where newspapers cost one dollar. Yet, imagine this shopper has a psychiatric condition rendering her so anxious that she cannot even try to buy anything. Regrettably, this agent does not have the option of buying anything, and so does not have the option of buying a newspaper. Yet it is true that if she chose to buy a newspaper, she would do so—it just so happens that her condition makes that choice unavailable to her. So CA is false.

Many have protested that this kind of example tells against the letter, but not the spirit, of CA. It may be proposed that CA should be restricted to 'psychologically possible' acts, and that some independent account of psychological possibility could be given. Relatedly, it might be proposed that CA gives an account of 'freedom of action' rather than 'freedom of will,' on some understanding of that distinction. I will shortly argue against these views and make the case that this simple counterexample indicates a problem with the very spirit of CA. At this point, however, I only wish to make the point that CA as stated is false, and to consider additional cases that make the same point.

Consider then the second counterexample. This is a case we have already considered: Frankfurt's case from the previous chapter. To repeat, in this case a person steals some money. A neuroscientist would have prevented her from deciding not to steal the money. As it happens, she decided to steal the money on her own, so the neuroscientist did not need to intervene. Earlier we noted that this is a counterexample to the principle that one is morally responsible for an act only if one has the option of doing otherwise. I now want to emphasize that, at least on one way of specifying the details of the case, it is also a counterexample to CA. It may be true that if the agent were to choose to not steal the money, she would not steal the money. It just so happens that the neuroscientist would prevent her from even choosing to not steal the money. Nonetheless, she does not have the option of not stealing the money—that is precisely the point that the example is designed to make.

In a way, this second counterexample is simply a variation on the first. The neuroscientist here functions in the same way as the psychiatric disorder surveyed in the previous counterexample, with the difference that the effects of the psychiatric disorder are actual while those of the neuroscientist are counterfactual. Nonetheless, the fundamental point in each case is the same: even though the act is in some sense physically available for the agent, it is not an option for her, in virtue of the constraints imposed (or possibly imposed, in the case of the neuroscientist) on her volitional psychology.

This second counterexample does, however, add at least one point to those made by the first. For the second counterexample is one in which having alternative options and being morally responsible come apart. When they do come apart, it turns out that CA tracks moral responsibility, rather than tracking options. This suggests that though CA may fail as an account of options, a related proposal might succeed as at least part of an account of moral responsibility. I will return to this point below.

The first two counterexamples are concerned with specific cases. The third is more general, and concerns kinds of agents. We should admit the possibility, I believe, of agents who have options yet whose psychology does not include anything that we might call a choice (or an intention, or a trying, or any volitional state at all). The argument for this is not merely that such beings are conceivable, though I believe they are conceivable, and it is significant that they are. The point is rather that such beings are, or have thought by some to be, actual.

There are two kinds of cases here. The first are those that are in some sense 'above' human beings. It may well be that an omnipotent being, if such there be, simply acts as she sees fit, without trying or choosing to act in a particular way. That is, it may be that volitional states are only appropriate for those beings whose powers are limited. A second case involves those beings that are 'below' human beings: for example, other mammals. It seems to be an empirical possibility that such beings do not have the cognitive sophistication to have volitional states but that they nonetheless act and have the option of acting in more than one way.[6]

---

[6] This is an application, to the realm of options, of H.P. Grice's highly instructive method of 'creature construction' (Grice, 1974).

What does CA say about such cases? It asks us to consider what would be the case if these agents who cannot choose did make choices. It may be that this yields an extensionally adequate result in certain cases,[7] but even if this is so, this last example seems to show that CA generally is wide of the mark. If certain agents do not and indeed cannot have options, then their options are not to be analyzed in terms of what they would do if they had volitional states that they could not even have.

This last point suggests, as the previous counterexamples also did, that CA is not a general analysis of options but is playing some other role altogether. The next section pursues the question of what it gets right, and what it gets wrong, and why, I argue, no analysis of this general form is adequate to the analysis of options.

2.3 The Appeal to Volition

We have now considered three challenges to the view that CA constitutes an analysis of what it is to have an option. Since these challenges have insisted, as noted above, on the letter of CA, it is natural to suppose that some more sophisticated formulation might address these worries. The attempt to do this remains one of the major research programs in the study of agentive modality. I will not attempt to survey and address every such analysis.[8] Rather, I want to raise some general concerns about the very foundations of this research program.

The first concern was already indicated in the discussion of the first counterexample, involving agents with pathological phobias that render them incapable of even choosing to act. The response considered there was one on which CA captures something that such an agent does have, namely 'freedom of action' as opposed to 'freedom of will,'[9] and perhaps

---

[7] For instance, it may be that all counterfactuals with impossible antecedent are true (Lewis, 1973), and that a divine being is essentially such that it does not make choices. Then CA predicts that such a being has every option whatsoever, which may in fact be true if that being is omnipotent. But here it is clear that the extensional adequacy of CA in this case is merely coincidental.

[8] See Maier (2020) for a more extensive survey of these issues.

[9] See Albritton (1985) for an insistence on this supposed distinction, and a forceful defense of the freedom of the will so understood.

24   J. T. Maier

that the former notion is the philosophically or anyhow metaphysically interesting notion here, and that CA or something like it gives a perfectly good analysis of that notion.

This approach, I believe, is unsound. When an agent has a certain act as an option, this will be the case in virtue of certain factors. Some of these will be physical or environmental. For instance, someone has the option of purchasing a newspaper partly in virtue of the presence of newspapers in the store and the presence of money in her pocket. Some of these factors, however, will be psychological. In the case at hand, they will be primarily negative, such as the absence of pathological anxiety. In other cases, they may be more substantive. Arguably few people have the option of meditating for 24 consecutive hours, though the merely physical conditions on this act are relatively thin. Generally, one has an option in virtue both of one's psychology and of non-psychological facts. In this respect, having an option is like knowledge, or for that matter like action itself.[10]

What then of the 'freedom of action,' or of 'physical opportunity'? I do not deny that one may define such notions in a rigorous way.[11] What I want to deny is that these notions have anything to do with the immediate objects of agents' deliberation. The objects of deliberation are options, and options have a psychological as well as a non-psychological element. CA is mistaken because it simply abstracts away from the psychological element of options, and thus goes awry in cases where the obstacle that confronts an agent is a psychological one.[12]

Options then, are not to be analyzed in terms of the counterfactual dependence of action on volition. At this point it is worth asking what CA does capture, if not the possession of options. Here it is worth

---

[10] On the symmetries between knowledge and action, see Williamson (2017).

[11] Although neither should we take it as unproblematic that we can define such notions. It may be that there is simply no unique solution to the question: what is left over of options, once one takes away their purely psychological element? On the problems of such philosophical subtractions, see Yablo (2014).

[12] This observation raises the prospect for a conjunctive analysis of options: perhaps having an option is a matter of satisfying some purely physical condition and being free of all psychological obstacles. The difficulty lies in articulating the nature of these physical conditions and absent psychological obstacles without appealing to the notion of having an option itself. The most serious attempt at doing this is developed in Peacocke (1999); a counterexample to that proposal is developed in Maier (2020).

considering our second counterexample. The agent in Frankfurt's case, who does not have the option of acting otherwise, nonetheless would do otherwise if she chose to. She is also morally responsible for what she actually does. One natural thought is that this is no coincidence: that doing what one chooses to do is not an account of options, but that it is part of an account of the conditions on moral responsibility.

Consider an agent who does what she chooses to do, and who would do whatever she chose to do. Such an agent is, in the philosophical sense, autonomous, or self-governing. Her acts are fully governed by her choices, in this world and in any other one. She is free, in at least one sense of that term. While the conditional analysis does constitute an analysis of options, it does constitute a compelling articulation of a certain kind of agentive ideal. It is this fact that explains, at least in part, the deep and lasting appeal of the conditional analysis.[13]

This is also a distinctly anthropocentric, or anyhow not entirely general, conception of self-governance. Beings who do not have volitions, being either too sophisticated for them or not sophisticated enough, may not sensibly be said to have their acts depend on their volitions. They may nonetheless have options, which are, on the present account, a far more general aspect of agency. This answers the third point made above, that there may be agents to whom CA does not even intelligibly apply. This is acceptable, and to be expected, if the appeal to volition is doing something other than giving an account of agents' options, which are our concern here.

2.4 The Modal Analysis

The last concern about CA was that it was too specific, drawing on facts about human psychology in its analysis of options. I responded to this concern by arguing that ultimately the conditional analysis was articulating a condition on responsible agency in creatures like ourselves, rather

---

[13] One finds versions of the conditional analysis defended by—among others—Hobbes (Hobbes & Bramhall, 1999), Locke (Locke, 1690/1996), Hume (Hume, 1748/2011), and Jonathan Edwards (Edwards, 1754/2009).

26   J. T. Maier

than an analysis of options. If we do want to give an analysis of options, however, this last criticism indicates that it much be more general in form.

A natural way of pursuing this generality is by offering a modal analysis of options. Begin with the observation that claims about an agents' options are, in some sense, claims about what is 'possible for' her. An agent has buying a newspaper as an option just in case it is possible for her to buy a newspaper—that claim is true for at least some sense of 'possible.' So a truly general analysis of options might take as its starting point the observations that options are a kind of possibility.

In much contemporary philosophy and linguistics, it is customary to understand claims about possibility and necessity in the framework of modality. In this framework, possibility and necessity are properly modeled as operators on propositions. Thus, a possibility claim is understood in terms of the claim that a certain proposition is possible. These operators are in turn understood semantically in terms of quantification over possible worlds, and accessibility relations between worlds: a proposition is possible just in case it is true at some accessible possible world, and necessary just in case it is true at every accessible possible world.[14]

How does this thought apply to the case of agents and their possibilities? Let us say that it is possible for some agent to buy a newspaper. On the proposal under consideration, it is natural to understand this claim in terms of the proposition that the agent buys a newspaper, and the possibility of that proposition, which is in turn understood in terms of existential quantification over possible worlds. What it is for it to be possible for the agent to buy a newspaper is for there to be an accessible possible world at which the agent buys a newspaper.

More generally, let the modal analysis of ability be the following claim:

(MA) S OPT α just in case there is an accessible possible world at which S does α

---

[14] Different accessibility relations will in turn be fitting for different kinds of possibility. For instance, a model in which accessibility is reflexive—that is, where every world can be accessed from itself—will be one in which the truth of a proposition suffices for its possibility. (If a proposition is true at a world and accessibility is reflexive there is an accessible possible world at which that proposition is true, namely that world itself.) A minimal modal logic, to be discussed presently, is one which holds for a model whatever the accessibility relations among worlds might be.

2 The Simplicity of Options   27

Unlike CA, MA is not so much an analysis as it is a family of analyses. Different members of this family will be distinguished by the accounts they give of the accessibility relation. To endorse MA is to endorse the view that there is some understanding of the accessibility relation that yields extensionally adequate results.

It is not obvious that this can be done, that there is any understanding of what the accessibility relation is that does not itself appeal to the idea of an option.[15] I want to waive that objection, however, and focus on an objection that applies to MA on any possible resolution of the accessibility relation. This objection is an objection against the very form of MA, and it indicates a fundamental asymmetry between options and possibility and necessity as these have been understood in the modal tradition.

The objection is due to Anthony Kenny (Kenny, 1976). Kenny considers a case like the following one.[16] An agent has a normal deck of cards before her. She has the option of pulling a card from the deck. As every card in the deck is red or black, she has the option of pulling a red or black card from the deck.[17] Yet she does not have the option of pulling a red card from the deck. When she is deliberating about what to do, pulling a red card should not be among her options. Her options are not so fine-grained as that. Rather, she has the option of pulling (or not pulling) a card, which may or may not turn out to be red. And the same point applies, by parity of reasoning, to pulling a black card.

This agent then has the option of pulling a black or a red card but does not have pulling a black card or pulling a red card as an option. This suggests a fundamental asymmetry between the principles that govern

---

[15] This objection to MA is developed in Maier (2015), who grants the extensional adequacy of MA but argues that it cannot constitute a reductive analysis of options, since it requires some such notion in order to define the accessibility relation that governs agentive modality. The present argument makes the more fundamental argument that MA fails to even be extensionally adequate.

[16] Kenny does not put matters in terms of options, but in other details the case is essentially his.

[17] This reasoning relies on the following principle, which we might call the Equivalence Principle:

If S OPT α, and S performs an act of type α just in case S performs an act of type β, then S OPT β

If we let α be 'pull a card from the deck' and β be 'pull a red or a black card from the deck,' then the Equivalence Principle in this case underwrites the reasoning given in the text. We will have reason to revisit the Equivalence Principle, which some philosophers seem to have doubted, though it does not seem at all plausible to defend MA by denying it in the case at hand.

28   J. T. Maier

options, on the one hand, and the logic of possibility in the modal tradition, on the other. There are many modal logics in this tradition, but the principle that possibility distributes over disjunction is an axiom of the weakest 'normal' modal logic K, where a normal modal logic is one whose semantics may be given in terms of quantification over individual possible worlds and accessibility relations among those worlds. It is this point that leads Kenny to observe: 'if we regard possible worlds semantics as making explicit what is involved in being a possibility, we must say that ability is not any kind of possibility' (Kenny, 1976, p. 140).[18]

Accordingly, this case provides a counterexample to the modal analysis of options MA. Consider an agent who has the option of picking a red or a black card. By MA, there is an accessible possible world at which she picks a red or a black card. At that world, she picks a red card or she picks a black card.[19] Without loss of generality, let us say that she picks a red card. Applying MA again, now in the opposite direction, it follows that she has the option of picking a red card. But this is precisely what is not the case.

This example, crucially, does not turn on any specifics of the case at issue. It indicates, as noted above, a fundamental asymmetry between the logic of options on the one hand and normal modal logics on the other. And this formal asymmetry, I will now argue, has grounds in the nature of agency itself.

---

[18] Note that the objection is not quite that distribution over disjunction fails for options. Disjunction is not even defined for options: disjunction is an operation on propositions, not on acts. The dialectic of the objection is somewhat more complicated. Assume, for reductio, that options can be modeled within the framework of possible worlds. Then the kind of possibility that corresponds to options would fail to distribute over disjunction. But possibility distributes over disjunction in any normal modal logic. Therefore, options cannot be modeled within the framework of possible worlds.

[19] This is perhaps the most vulnerable premise of Kenny's argument. Might we not instead say that there are many accessible worlds at which she picks a card—at some of these it is red, and at some of these it is black—but that there is no 'fact of the matter' about whether the card she picks at some accessible world is red or black? To make this claim is to depart from a model of possibility in terms of accessibility relations among individual worlds and to move to a model of possibility in terms of relations to sets of worlds (or, alternately, a model of accessibility relations between individuals worlds combined with supervaluation over claims about individual worlds, in the manner of the treatment of conditional excluded middle in Stalnaker (1980)). This is a marked departure from the normal modal logics considered in this chapter. We will revisit the prospects for this strategy in more detail in the next chapter.

2.5 The Limits of Control

Michael Bratman (Bratman, 1987) observes that practical reason, crucially, leaves many things open. Often there is more than one way of executing our plans. If I plan to go to the library, there may be more than one way to go there, and part of the task of practical reason is to 'fill in' my plan by specifying what way I will take. I may also specify whether I will go by foot or by bike, how fast I will travel, what clothes I will wear, and so forth.

At some point, however, the specification will give out. Though there are more specific ways of executing my plan, I do not select among them. Sometimes this will be because of simple indifference: I do not care precisely how fast I travel to the library, so I will set out towards the library and figure out my pace as I go along, rather than deciding it in advance.

Sometimes, however, the specification of my plans faces a more fundamental limit: I am not in a position to specify my plan any further because I do not control the execution of my plan at so fine a grain. There is a difference between traveling to the library at exactly five miles an hour and just a little more quickly than that, but the measures by which I set my pace do not discriminate between these. If I do specify a rate at which I will travel to the library, then I can at most specify an interval of rates, and the actual rate that I will travel is some precise value within that range. I do travel at that rate, but traveling at that rate is not part of my plan.[20]

When we turn from plans to options, the situation is much the same. I have the option of traveling to the library by foot, or of traveling to the library by bike, but for some very precise rate, I do not have the option of traveling to the library at exactly that rate.[21] I have, at best, the option of traveling to the library at some rate within a certain interval, say at approximately five miles per hour.

---

[20] If I travel at some particular rate, I do so intentionally, but it does not follow that I intended to travel at exactly that rate. On the difference between what we intend to do and what we do intentionally, see also Bratman (1987).

[21] We can of course imagine cases where I do have this as an option, where I have sufficient control over my pace or access to sufficiently accurate timing mechanisms. I am stipulating that we are considering a case where such elements are absent.

30   J. T. Maier

Similarly, in the case discussed earlier, I have the option of picking a red card or a black card, but I do not have the option of picking a red card or the option of picking a black card. We can now see that this is not an unusual case, but an instance of a very general phenomenon of practical reason. The phenomenon is that agents plan and deliberate at a certain level of abstraction, more coarse-grained than the world itself. And the origin of this phenomenon lies in the fact that agents control the world, but control it only imperfectly. They are in a position to bring about more or less determinate outcomes without being in a position to settle precisely what form those outcomes take.

It is these limits of agentive control that give rise to the failure of the modal analysis. Possibility as it is conceived of in the modal tradition is determinate: if some proposition is possible, then it is possible at some possible world, and possible worlds are maximally specific ways for things to be. Generality on this conception is arrived at through abstraction from specific realizations. For example, the proposition that someone picks a card is possible is true in virtue of that proposition being true at many specific worlds, at some of which the card is red and at some of which the card is black.

The generality involved in agency, however, is sui generis. It is not arrived at from abstraction from more specific scenarios, for there are no such scenarios. What there exist are options, and options are inherently somewhat specific, but not entirely so. They are as specific as the control that agents have, which is almost always imperfect.[22] It is in virtue of this metaphysical fact that, formally, options fail to distribute over disjunction in the way that possibility, on the modal conception, does. And this asymmetry, in turn, generates the failure of MA.

---

[22] Omnipotent beings may constitute an exception. Discussions of omnipotence typically concern the power of omnipotent beings to perform tasks much greater than can any finite being. A less noted aspect of omnipotence—which we might call 'omniprecision'—is the power of beings to perform infinitely precise tasks, such as having the power of lifting exactly r kilograms for any real number r. MA may well be extensionally adequate when applied to an omniprecise being. It fails as an analysis of options generally because beings such as ourselves have options, and we are not omniprecise.

On the present account, we might accept that MA is extensionally adequate for an agent who exercises precise control over the world. MA fails taken as an analysis of options generally, but it might succeed if taken as a description of the options of being of unlimited precision.

There is a still more general perspective from which to frame this issue. One might object to the possible worlds framework, especially on its literal interpretation advocated in Lewis (1986), to fail to capture agentive freedom. If facts about what I can do are reducible to facts about what I simply do at a variety of possible worlds, then facts about my freedom seem to be lost, since these essentially concern acts that I do not perform.[23]

The present argument may be thought of as a formal development of this admittedly impressionistic objection. Facts about what I do, even facts about what I do across the plurality of possible worlds, are maximally specific facts. In contrast, facts about what I can do—my options— are not specific in this way. So the present argument lends support to the idea that claims about my options are not to be reduced to claims about my acts, including claims about my possible acts. Options are a distinctive phenomenon and call for their own account.

2.6 The Simple View

There is a view that accepts with equanimity the failure of CA and MA. This is what I will call the simple view of options. On this view, there is no independently specifiable condition C such that S OPT α just in case α satisfies C.[24] On CA and MA there is such a condition. The simple view, which I endorse, holds that there is not.

The simple view is simple twice over. First, it is simple in that it holds options to be analytically simple, not susceptible to further analysis. Second, it is simple insofar it does not involve the substantive views of options involved in CA and MA. The simple view is, in this sense, metaphysically minimalist—it holds that there are options, but that there is no further account of what it is to have an option.[25]

---

[23] This objection is in the neighborhood of the objections from indifference and from non-arbitrariness considered in Lewis (1986, pp. 123–133).

[24] A condition is independently specifiable just in case it does not itself include the option relation.

[25] In another sense, the simple view has a more copious ontology than other views, for it does not reduce options to anything else. A full inventory of the world must therefore include, among other things, the options of agents.

It is important to be clear on the commitments of this view. The simple view holds that there is no condition satisfying both criteria. It does not hold that it is certain or provable that there is no such condition. Certain philosophical arguments, such as G.E. Moore's 'Open Question' argument (Moore, 1903), purport to establish these stronger kinds of claims. The simple view is the weaker view that there is in fact no such condition.

As such, endorsement of the simple view does not require us to canvas every possible analysis of options and show that it is mistaken. Rather, the systematic failure of certain prominent attempts at analyzing options gives us reason to believe that the simple view is true. The simple view is an analytic hypothesis that is supported by strong, though defeasible, grounds.

While the present discussion may be the first to explicitly endorse the simple view of options, something like this view is congenial to many approaches to agency. It fits well, for example, with discussions in decision theory that help themselves to a notion of options and then proceed to frame decision problems in terms of options. This kind of methodological primitivism is closely allied to the metaphysical primitivism involved in the simple view. The simple view may already be the unofficial ideology of all those who recognize the significance of options as well as the difficulty of analyzing them.

Why, if the simple view is so widespread, have analyses of options such as CA and MA been so prominent in philosophical discussions? Partly this has been because philosophers have been sensitive to the arguments that can be brought against primitivist views generally and against the simple view in particular. One of the tasks of the remainder of this chapter will be articulating and responding to those arguments.

But, in addition to those negative motivations, there have also been positive attractions to analyses of options. Many authors, for instance, have supposed that endorsement of CA is the best way to reconcile agentive freedom with the possibility of determinism. Other authors have endorsed MA as part of a more general program of understanding the semantics and metaphysics of modality in terms of quantification over possible worlds. In short, philosophers have generally endorsed analyses of options—and so rejected the simple view—not merely for the sake of doing so, but in pursuit of some larger philosophical program.

A central motivation for the endorsement of CA is the project of reconciling agentive freedom with the possible truth of determinism. On one development of this thought, it proceeds as follows. Certain arguments purport to show that agents having options is incompatible with the truth of determinism.[26] Most philosophers agree, however, that the truth of certain counterfactuals is compatible with the truth of determinism.[27] If options are analyzable in terms of counterfactuals, as CA, then these arguments for the incompatibility of options and determinism must be somehow sophistical.

If something like this project is one's motivation for endorsing CA, then one will be reluctant to accept the simple view merely in light of the counterexamples adduced above. I believe that the best response to this consideration is not to offer still more counterexamples, but to show how that advocate of the simple view might respond to arguments for the incompatibility of options and determinism. Indeed, as I will argue in Chap. 7, it is the simple view that grounds the best defense of compatibilism about options and determinism, a view that I will call fundamental compatibilism, as it turns essentially on the fundamentality of options.[28]

A different project has typically motivated MA. This is the project of giving a general account of possibility and necessity in terms of quantification over possible worlds. This project is a semantic as well as a metaphysical one, and it has been a central research program of analytic philosophy and formal semantics of recent decades, most of all in the work of David Lewis and Angelika Kratzer. MA may be thought of as a

---

[26] As noted earlier, strictly these arguments concern only the unexercised options of agents. By the lights of what I will shortly dub the Performance Principle, an agent has the option of performing any act that she actually performs. Arguments for the incompatibility of options and determinism, which we will consider explicitly in Chap. 7, concern only those options that an agent does not perform.

[27] If anything, it is indeterminism that appears to threaten the truth of ordinary counterfactuals; see Hawthorne (2005).

[28] Another consideration is that, as observed in van Inwagen (1983, p. 121) any argument for the incompatibility of determinism and proper options is also, in virtue of that, an argument against CA. Therefore, if one's aim is to answer these arguments, an appeal to CA threatens to be dialectically ineffective. The simple view, by contrast, provides a more fundamental grounds for questioning these arguments.

34   J. T. Maier

specific application of this much more general program to the case of agentive modality.

I believe that this project fails as a general account of modality, and that agency is one of the rocks on which it founders.[29] In this respect the attitude of the present argument towards this project is different from its attitude towards compatibilism. Compatibilism should be upheld, while this more local and recent project—the possible worlds approach, we might call it—should be rejected, precisely in light of its failure to capture the possibility that is distinctive to agency.[30]

Nonetheless, the advocates of MA offer a systematic semantics for agentive modality, and they may reasonably ask how this is to be done on a view that does not give any positive account of what it is to have an option. The answer to this view is that options themselves should figure in the semantics of expressions of agentive modality, in particular in the semantics of the modal predicate 'is able' and its cognates. That semantics will be developed in the next chapter. In that sense, just as the argument for the simple view against CA will be completed only in Chap. 7, so will the argument for the simple view against MA be completed only in Chap. 3.

In short, most authors have advocated analyses of options because of the role that those analyses play in certain philosophical projects, and a comprehensive response to their views should not only give counterexamples to their analyses, but also show how their projects can be pursued on a view that takes options to be simple. That is the kind of response that will be developed in the discussion to follow.

2.7   An Explanatory Challenge

One way of challenging the simple view, then, is to argue that it cannot carry out the various philosophical projects that analyses of options have been expected to carry out. The response to that challenge will occupy

---

[29] Another is the need to give an account of essence; see Fine (1994).
[30] The thought that the modal approach is inadequate to agentive modality, on purely formal grounds, is developed in Maier (2018).

2 The Simplicity of Options   35

much of the rest of the discussion. There is also, however, a more direct challenge to the simple view, which bears considering here.

The challenge proceeds as follows. When someone has an option, this will typically be in virtue of certain other facts, ones that do not themselves involve options. For example, when someone has the option of buying a newspaper, this will typically be the case partly in virtue of facts about the money that she has at hand and the availability of newspapers.

Generalizing, we can observe that the options that agents have generally depend on facts that do not themselves involve options, and ultimately on physical facts. Indeed, the following principle seems plausible. Consider two worlds that are wholly alike physically. If an agent has an option in one of these worlds, then that agent has that same option in the other of them. That is to say that options supervene on the physical.

This supervenience principle seems to me exceedingly plausible. Where then is the objection? It runs as follows. If options were analyzable in terms of more basic facts, then we might have an explanation of why they supervene on the physical. For, the thought goes, the analyzing terms (volition, for example, in CA), might be further analyzed, and these in turn might be further analyzed, until we reach fundamental physical facts.[31] If, however, options are not unanalyzable, then the supervenience of options on the physical must be taken as an inexplicable fact, and this is unacceptable.

The proper response to this argument is to point out how widely it applies. Moral and normative facts supervene on the physical (McPherson, 2012). So too, many philosophers hold, do phenomenal facts.[32] Indeed, closer to home, action and agency themselves plausibly supervene on the physical.[33] Yet for each of these, a simple view has some plausibility. There is no special inexplicability, then, in the simple view of options. Rather, the advocate of this objection to the simple view is demanding an explanation where, on balance, it is not reasonable to expect for one to be given.

---

[31] For a thorough discussion of the physicalist project and how it might be understood, see Stoljar (2010).

[32] This doctrine is elegantly explained in Chalmers (1996), though Chalmers himself denies it.

[33] While this observation seems uncontentious, its implications may remain unappreciated. See Turner (2009) for an argument that the incompatibilist about options and determinism is required to deny a certain kind of supervenience thesis.

Insofar as this argument from inexplicability has special purchase against the simple view of options, it rests on a failure to acknowledge that options are—like normativity and phenomenal consciousness—good candidates to be fundamental features of the world as we find it. There may indeed be some mystery in the fact that these features supervene on the physical yet are irreducible to it, but if there is indeed a problem here it is not a problem about options in particular but a problem for fundamental metaphysics generally.

While the supervenience of options on the physical does not tell against the simple view, it is an important datum about options and how they hang together with our conception of the world more generally. This is a topic to which we will return.

2.8 The Performance Principle

The simple view holds that there is no condition that is both necessary and sufficient for having an option, and that does not itself involve having an option. Yet the simple view is compatible with there being necessary conditions of this kind for having an option, and with there being sufficient conditions of this kind. On the present view, there are two such conditions, one of them sufficient for having an option, and one of them a necessary consequence of having an option.

This section will concern the sufficient condition, which I will call the Performance Principle:

If S performs an act of type α, then S OPT α[34]

For example, if someone raises her arm, then she has the option of raising her arm and, if someone hits a bull's eye, then she has the option of pulling a bull's eye.

---

[34] Note that, as before, Greek letters such as α denotes acts, where these are understood as act types rather than act tokens. The acts that one performs, on the other hand, are particular happenings or act tokens, which may fall under more than one act type. (For instance, one may, with a single gesture, both raise one's arm and alert the police.) The performance principle is stated as it is to capture this aspect of the ontology of action.

2 The Simplicity of Options   37

To see why this principle is true, it is helpful to reflect on the platitudes that we invoked when introducing the idea of an option in the first place. An agent's options are the acts among which she deliberates. They are the acts that figure in a description of her choice situation. It is this deliberative role of options that gives them their central place in the theory of agency.

We can now bring these platitudes to bear on the performance principle. Consider an agent who performs an improbable act—say, hitting a bull's eye in darts. Was this among her options? Yes. In retrospect, it is one that it would have been proper for her to deliberate about.[35] It is an act that ought to have been included in a decision-theoretic framing of her choice situation. There are other things we might say about this option, for example that she did not know she had this option. But, given the deliberative role of options, it was an option that she had.[36]

This aspect of options is implicit, I believe, in natural language. Austin remarks that there is a sense of 'ability' such that 'it follows merely from the premise that he does it, that he has the ability to do it, according to ordinary English' (Austin, 1956). It is this sense that captures the way in which performing an act is sufficient for having the option to perform it. There is also, however, a sense of 'ability' on which performance is not sufficient for ability. This latter sense of 'ability,' and its connection to options, will be discussed and explained in the next chapter.

2.9   The Possibility Principle

The performance principle is a sufficient condition for having an option. There is also a necessary condition. This is a condition such that someone has an option only if it obtains. This is what I will call the Possibility Principle.

---

[35] This is a normative claim and, as the subsequent discussion indicates, it is a claim of objective normativity. That is, it is not a claim about what she ought to have deliberated above relative to what she knew, but about what she ought to have deliberated about simpliciter.

[36] In general, as noted in the previous chapter, options are not epistemically transparent: from the fact that someone has α as an option, it does not follow that she knows that she has α as an option.

This principle, too, is marked by natural language. Earlier we observed that an agent's options may be described in terms of what is 'possible for' her. One possible explanation for this fact is that claims about agents' options are simply modal claims, and admit of an analysis in terms of quantification over possible worlds. That was the proposal MA, which we rejected.

The argument against MA, however, was limited in its scope. It showed that options could not be analyzed in modal terms because there were acts that an agent performed at some possible world that she did not have the option of performing. That is, one direction of the analytic hypothesis made by MA fails. The other direction, however—that claims about options entail certain claims about possibility—was not threatened.

It is this claim, I suggest, that marks a necessary condition on having an option, or the Possibility Principle:

If S OPT α, then there is a possible world at which S performs an act of type α

This principle, I suggest, captures the core truth expressed by MA. There is a deep affinity between options and possibility, as expressed in the idioms of natural language. Yet options cannot be analyzed in terms of possible worlds, for the reasons already given. These two facts are reconciled by the thought that claims about possible worlds are implied by, though they do not themselves imply, claims about options.

An interesting question is whether the Possibility Principle may be further constrained. According to the Possibility Principle, someone's having an act as an option implies that there is a possible world where she performs that act. It places no restriction on what that world is. We may then consider more restricted principles. Does having an act as an option imply, for instance, that there is a historically possible world—a world with the same past as our own—at which one performs that act? I will eventually argue that it does not necessarily imply this. It is only in its unrestricted form that the possibility principle expresses an exceptionless truth about options. More restricted versions of this principle—versions with which the possibility principle is easily confused—are more contentious, and are no part of the present argument. Indeed, the careless conflation of the valid Possibility Principle with more restricted, invalid, principles has been a foundational error in the theory of agentive modality, which the present discussion aims to set right.

Bibliography

Albritton, R. (1985). Freedom of Will and Freedom of Action. *Proceedings and Addresses of the American Philosophical Association, 59*(2), 239–251.

Austin, J. L. (1956). Ifs and Cans. *Proceedings of the British Academy, 42*, 109–132.

Baier, A. C. (1970). Act and Intent. *The Journal of Philosophy, 67*(19), 648–658.

Bostrom, N. (2014). *Superintelligence: Paths, Dangers, Strategies.* Oxford University Press.

Bratman, M. (1987). *Intention, Plans, and Practical Reason.* Harvard University Press.

Chalmers, D. J. (1996). *The Conscious Mind: In Search of a Fundamental Theory.* Oxford University Press.

Edwards, J. (1754/2009). *The Freedom of the Will* (P. Ramsey, ed.). Yale University Press.

Fine, K. (1994). Essence and Modality. *Philosophical Perspectives, 8*, 1–16.

Goldman, A. I. (1970). *Theory of Human Action.* Prentice-Hall.

Grice, P. (1974). Method in Philosophical Psychology (From the Banal to the Bizarre). *Proceedings and Addresses of the American Philosophical Association, 48*, 23–53.

Hawthorne, J. (2005). Chance and Counterfactuals. *Philosophy and Phenomenological Research, 70*(2), 396–405.

Hobbes, T., & Bramhall, J. (1999). *Hobbes and Bramhall on Liberty and Necessity* (V. Chappell, ed.). Cambridge University Press.

Hume, D. (1748/2011). *An Enquiry Concerning Human Understanding.* Simon & Brown.

Kenny, A. J. P. (1976). *Will, Freedom, and Power.* Barnes & Noble Books.

Lewis, D. K. (1973). *Counterfactuals.* Blackwell.

Lewis, D. K. (1986). *On the Plurality of Worlds.* Wiley-Blackwell.

Locke, J. (1690/1996). *An Essay Concerning Human Understanding* (K. P. Winkler, ed.). Hackett Publishing Company.

Maier, J. (2015). The Agentive Modalities. *Philosophy and Phenomenological Research, 90*(1), 113–134.

Maier, J. (2018). Ability, Modality, and Genericity. *Philosophical Studies, 175*(2), 411–428.

Maier, J. (2020). Abilities. In E. N. Zalta (Ed.), *The Stanford Encyclopedia of Philosophy*. Metaphysics Research Lab, Stanford University.

Mandelkern, M., Schultheis, G., & Boylan, D. (2017). Agentive Modals. *Philosophical Review, 126*(3), 301–343.

McPherson, T. (2012). Ethical Non-Naturalism and the Metaphysics of Supervenience. In R. Shafer-Landau (Ed.), *Oxford Studies in Metaethics Vol 7*. Oxford University Press.

Moore, G. E. (1903). *Principia Ethica*. Cambridge University Press.

Peacocke, C. (1999). *Being Known*. Clarendon Press.

Stalnaker, R. C. (1968). A Theory of Conditionals. In N. Rescher (Ed.), *Studies in Logical Theory (American Philosophical Quarterly Monographs 2)* (pp. 98–112). Blackwell.

Stalnaker, R. C. (1980). A Defense of Conditional Excluded Middle. In W. Harper, R. C. Stalnaker, & G. Pearce (Eds.), *IFS*. Springer Netherlands.

Steward, H. (2012). *A Metaphysics for Freedom*. Oxford University Press.

Stoljar, D. (2010). *Physicalism*. Routledge.

Turner, J. (2009). The Incompatibility of Free Will and Naturalism. *Australasian Journal of Philosophy, 87*(4), 565–587.

van Inwagen, P. (1983). *An Essay on Free Will*. Oxford University Press.

Williamson, T. (2017). Acting on Knowledge. In J. A. Carter, E. C. Gordon, & B. Jarvis (Eds.), *Knowledge First: Approaches in Epistemology and Mind*. Oxford University Press.

Yablo, S. (2014). *Aboutness*. Princeton University Press.

3

The Analysis of Ability

3.1 Options and Abilities

The previous chapter articulated a framework for thinking about agents' options, which are the fundamental notion for understanding the kind of possibility that is distinctive to agency.

Much of the contemporary and historical literature on agency and possibility is not, however, framed in terms of options. Instead, it is framed in terms of agents' abilities. The purpose of this chapter is to give an account of agents' abilities in terms of options.

This account will serve several purposes. First, it will show how to understand familiar puzzles about ability—puzzles that have been with us, in one form or another, at least since Aristotle—in terms of options. Second, it will show how those puzzles can be clarified and, to some degree, resolved by an appeal to agents' options. As such, it will be a demonstration of the utility of a framework of options in making clear the nature of agents and their possibilities.

Finally, it will show ability to be a comparatively superficial aspect of the theory of agency, in the following sense. Ability dominates our thought and talk about agency and possibility, but it turns out to be, on inspection, a highly context-sensitive and linguistically dependent

© The Author(s), under exclusive license to Springer Nature Switzerland AG 2022   **41**
J. T. Maier, *Options and Agency*, https://doi.org/10.1007/978-3-031-10243-1_3

3.2 'Able' and Ability

What is it for an agent to have an ability? That is, what is it for some agent to be able to do something—for instance, to be able to build a house? The metaphysical force of this question can best be appreciated when we consider the case where someone is not actually building a house. When someone who is able to build a house but is not actually now building a house—a carpenter, say—wherein does her ability reside? Aristotle writes:

> There are some, e.g. the Megaric school, who say that a thing only has potency when it functions, and that when it is not functioning it has no potency. E.g., they say that a man who is not building cannot build, but only the man who is building, and at the moment when he is building; and similarly in the other cases. It is not difficult to see the absurd consequences of this theory. (Metaphysics, Theta 3; Makin, 2006)

But, if we reject this 'absurd' theory, then what should we say about ability instead?

This chapter works out an answer to these questions. It begins by framing our question in the formal, rather than the material, mode. Let us not ask, just yet, what it is for someone (say, Sam) to have an ability (say, to build a bookshelf). Let us instead ask, under what conditions is the following sentence true:

(1) Sam is able to build a bookshelf

The project of giving a semantics for (1) is not quite the same as the project of giving an account of ability, but the projects are sufficiently intertwined that it makes sense to begin our inquiry into ability by devoting some attention to (1). Indeed, as I will eventually argue, the subtleties of (1) are sufficiently complicated that once we get a clear view of (1), we will have untangled most of the perplexities of ability as well.

The view of (1) that I will advocate builds on the framework of the previous chapter. We should give a semantics for (1) in terms of Sam's options. More generally, ability-ascriptions may be modeled as ways of talking about an agent's options. Moving from the formal back to the material mode, we may say that an agent's abilities depend, ultimately, on what her options are. Ability is the shadow cast by ability-ascriptions, and ability-ascriptions are to be understood in terms of options. Options, then, remain at the foundations of agency in its modal aspect.

3.3 The Ascription View

To appreciate the complexity of (1), and the subtlety of the relationship between ability and its ascription, it is helpful to consider an exceedingly simple view of the semantics of (1), and see why it is wrong. This view has not been advocated by any contemporary author, though views close to it appear in the philosophical literature and it is certainly a natural view to take, though ultimately, as will be shown, a mistaken view.[1]

The view is this. Say that there are such things as abilities, and their extension is something like what it is supposed to be. That is, most carpenters have the ability to build a bookshelf, and most non-carpenters lack that ability. Most people living in France have the ability to speak French, and most people living outside of France lack that ability. And so forth.

The Ascription View is then the following. There are abilities, and sentences of the form 'S is able to A' are simply ascriptions of such abilities. A sentence such as (1) is true just in case Sam has a certain ability, namely the ability to build a bookshelf, and it is false otherwise.

This view is simplicity itself. 'Able'-sentences are in key respects transparent to the underlying facts about ability. The philosopher of ability can sensibly move past sentences such as (1) and consider abilities in their own right, as the function of (1) is nothing more than the ascription of an ability.

This view makes the correct judgments in many cases. Nonetheless it is false. Consider:

---

[1] A view that bears some similarities to the view advanced here is the semantics for 'can' defended in Vetter (2013).

44   J. T. Maier

(2) Simone is able to speak French

Let us say that (2) is spoken when Simone is sedated for dental surgery, such that she cannot move her tongue. In virtue of that temporary impairment, Simone is unable to speak French. So (2) is false. Nonetheless Pierre retains the ability to speak French. That is an ability that does not come and go in response to sedation, sleep, or other such factors. So the view that (2) is the ascription of an ability is to be rejected. For, if (2) were an ascription of an ability, (2) would be true in the case described. But (2) is, in the circumstances described, false.

Consider also:

(3) Sebastian is able to speak Japanese

Let us say that (3) is spoken when Sebastian is equipped with an automatic translator, which translates his (English) speech into Japanese so that he can be understood while traveling in Japan. In such a case, (3) is true. Nonetheless, Sebastian does not have the ability to speak Japanese. That is an ability that is not acquired simply by the temporary use of an automatic translator. So the view that (3) is the ascription of an ability is to be rejected. For, if (3) were an ascription of an ability, (3) would be false in the case described. But it is not.

The argument of this subsection is that sentences of the form 'S is able to A'—that is, sentences such as (1), (2), and (3)—cannot be understood as ascriptions of ability, at least not if abilities are roughly what we ordinarily imagine them to be, for their truth (falsity) comes apart from the presence (absence) of abilities as we ordinarily understand them. If we want a semantics for sentences such as (1), (2), and (3), we require a different approach.[2]

---

[2] There is an important objection to the argument of this section that deserves careful attention. The objection is this. We should distinguish between sentences of the form 'S is able to A' and sentences of the form 'S has the ability to A.' I have been moving back and forth between these two sentences. But once we focus clearly on sentences of the form 'S has the ability to A,' the Ascription View may be salvaged. That is, the Ascription View might be the correct view of these sentences, even if it is false as a view of 'able'-sentences. Indeed, I have been implicitly accepting this view in the metalanguage, in saying that the agents in question retain their abilities even in situations where they are not able to act in certain ways.

I respond to this view in Sect. 3.9. There I extend the present semantics to 'ability'-sentences and argue, against this objection, for a unified account of 'able'-sentences and 'ability'-sentences. This is something that the present account, unlike the Ascription View, is in a position to deliver.

3.4 The Modal View

The Ascription View, while it is perhaps our natural untutored view of sentences such as (1), is not the default view of sentences such as (1) in contemporary semantics. Instead, sentences making claims about what an agent is able to do are to be understood in terms of an operator on sentences that do not involve such claims. This kind of view is developed with great force in Kratzer (1981) for the case of the modal auxiliary 'can,' but it is naturally extended to the modal predicate 'is able' as well.

To begin, consider again:

(1) Sam is able to build a bookshelf

We might think of (1) as involving two constituents: an underlying amodal sentence S—claiming, roughly, that Sam builds a bookshelf—and a modal operator on that sentence. Following Kratzer, we will take this to be a modal operator $\diamond$, understood as an existential quantifier over possible worlds. We then understand the semantics of (1) in terms of a sentence such as: $\diamond S$. And we understand this sentence in turn in terms of existential quantification over possible worlds: it is true just when there is a possible world of a certain kind at which Sam builds a bookshelf. What kind of world? Roughly, a world that is compatible with the facts that are being held fixed in the conversational context, and which is as good as any other with regard to the standards imposed by the conversational context.[3]

This view of the semantics of sentences such as (1) may be regarded as the dominant one in contemporary semantics. Nonetheless, it appears to face a couple of serious objections.

First, there is Kenny's objection. In Chap. 2 we considered it in the material mode as an objection to a modal analysis of options, while now we may reconsider it in the formal mode as an objection to a modal semantics for 'able'-sentences. Consider Sue, who is about to pick a random card from a deck. The following is generally true:

---

[3] These two conditions on the possible world describe what Kratzer (1981) terms the *modal base* and the *ordering source*, respectively.

(4) Sue is able to pick a red card or a black card

On the modal semantics, (4) is true just in case there is a world at which Sue picks a red card or a black card. Call that world w. At w, either Sue picks a black card or she picks a red card. Then, relative to exactly the same conversational context, w ensures the truth of at least one of the following:

(5) Sue is able to pick a red card
(6) Sue is able to pick a black card

But we can imagine scenarios where (4) is true yet neither (5) nor (6) is true. This will be the normal case, where Sue is able to pick cards but not able to pick cards of a particular color (this is the sort of ability that some card sharks might have, but that Sue lacks). So the modal semantics cannot accommodate this simple observation about 'able' and disjunction.

A second objection is developed in Mandelkern et al. (2017). The objection is the following. Consider someone, Shane, tossing a dart at a dartboard. Shane is able to play darts, but beyond that he has no special skills or training in the game; he loses as often as he wins. In the normal case, there is a possible world compatible with the facts that we are holding fixed (facts about Shane's physiology and psychology, facts about the dartboard in question, and so forth) that is as good as any other with respect our conversational background, at which Shane hits the bull's eye. This is just to say that there is an accessible and perfectly unsurprising world at which Shane hits the bull's eye. Still more informally, this is just to say that Shane might well his the bull's eye. Nonetheless, consider:

(7) Shane is able to hit the bull's eye

For all we have just said, (7) is false. Shane is a mediocre darts player, and as such does not have the ability to hit the bull's eye. It is true that he might sometimes hit it—but that just shows that there is more to being able than the possibility of success, at least when possibility is understood in the standard framework of modal semantics.

Both objections have a common core, which I would describe as follows. One's abilities concern the acts that are *within one's power*. It is not within Sue's power to pick a card of a given color, and it is not within

Shane's power to hit the bull's eye. That is why (5), (6), and (7) are, in the circumstances described, false. The modal view does not have the resources to accommodate this idea of what is, and what is not, within an agent's power. To give a correct semantics for 'able'-sentences, we will need to avail ourselves of a framework that does have those resources.

3.5   An Equivocation on 'Able'

In criticizing the Ascription View and the Modal View, I have focused on cases where our judgments about 'able'-sentences are confident. To move towards an alternative view, it will be helpful to consider a case where our judgments are more equivocal.

Consider again a darts player, Sasha. Sasha, like Shane, is a mediocre darts player. On some occasion, however, she does in fact hit the bull's eye. Consider the following sentence, spoken on that occasion:

(8) Sasha was able to hit the bull's eye

Is this sentence true, or is it not?[4]

Here, roughly, is the argument that it is true. She did hit the bull's eye, and she did so knowingly and intentionally. If what we are able to do is what is in our power, then Sasha was certainly able to hit the bull's eye on that occasion. After all, she did it!

Here, roughly, is the argument that it is not. Recall that Sasha is, with respect to darts, just like Shane. And recall that we judged, in rejecting (7), that Shane is not able to hit the bull's eye. So Sasha, being a mediocre darts player, is not able to hit the bull's eye either. So (8) is false as well. The fact that Sasha just so happens to have had some luck on this occasion does not make a difference to her abilities.

---

[4] Note that (8) involves the past tense. This is crucial to generating the ambiguity, for consider:

(8a) Sasha is able to hit the bull's eye

It is not clear that (8a) has a reading on which it is clearly true. From the fact that Sasha just hit the bull's eye, one might argue, nothing follows from what she is now able to do. This interaction between tense and 'able' is something we want for our considered semantics to explain, and I will offer such an explanation in what follows.

I think both arguments are entirely compelling on their own terms. As they cannot both be true, we must accept that (8) has two readings. I do not want to say that 'able' is ambiguous, in the way that term is sometimes used in the philosophical literature, to denote two terms with distinct semantics that stand only in a relation of homophony. Rather, I propose that 'able'-sentences systematically have two readings, which I will call their *specific* and their *general* reading. 'Able'-sentences admit of a *dual aspect* semantics, and the double aspect of these sentences will be shown to be the genesis of many of the perplexities in the semantics of 'able'-sentences and the metaphysics of ability.

3.6 'Able': The Specific Reading

What is the specific reading of 'able'-sentences? On this reading, these sentences simply ascribe options. That is, consider once more:

(1) Sam is able to build a bookshelf

On its specific reading, (1) is true just in case Sam now has building a bookshelf as an option—as will be the case, for instance, if he is a competent carpenter with all the requisite materials at hand. Conversely, on the specific reading of (1), it is false just in case Sam does not have this act as an option. For instance, if Sam simply does not have a hammer, nails, or lumber, then there is a sense in which (1) is simply false—even if there may be, and I in fact will argue there is, another sense in which (1) is true.

More generally, consider some 'able'-sentence:

S is able to A

Where 'S' is a name denoting some agent S and 'A' is a phrase denoting some act α. I propose that, *on its specific reading*, this sentence is true just in case:

S OPT α

This is not the whole story of the semantics for 'able'-sentences, but it is half of the story, and it accounts for some of the difficulties we have already encountered.

3 The Analysis of Ability 49

First, it explains why, against the Ascription View, there is a reading on which (2) is false:

(2) Simone is able to speak French

Recall that we were evaluating (2) relative to a case where Simone was a competent French speaker under the influence of dental sedation. In such a case, because of the sedation, Simone does not have the option of speaking, and so does not have the option of speaking French. Thus the present view can provide a sense in which (2) is false, which the Ascription View cannot do.

Similarly, it explains why, against the Ascription View, there is a reading on which (3) is true:

(3) Sebastian is able to speak Japanese

Recall that we were evaluating (3) relative to the case where Sebastian is a monolingual English speaker possessed of a highly accurate Japanese-voice-translation device. In such a case, because of his device, Sebastian has speaking Japanese as an option. Thus the present view can provide a sense in which (3) is true, which the Ascription View cannot do.

Second, it explains why, against the Modal View, why there is at least one reading on which (4) is true without either (5) or (6) being true:

(4) Sue is able to pick a red card or a black card
(5) Sue is able to pick a red card
(6) Sue is able to pick a black card

On its specific reading, (4) is true just in case Sue has a certain option: the option of picking a red or a black card. This does not, in general, entail that she has the option of picking a red card or the option of picking a black card. Whether she has these further options will depend, as discussed in Chap. 2, on how fine-grained her control is. Therefore the truth of (4), on its specific reading, does not suffice for the truth of (5) or (6), on their specific readings.

Third, it explains why, against the Modal View, (7) is not true:

(7) Shane is able to hit the bull's eye

Recall that we were evaluating (7) relative to the case where Shane is a mediocre darts player with sufficient materials (dart and dartboard) at hand. We said that while it might be possible that Shane hits the bull's eye, he is not able to hit the bull's eye. The present view vindicates this judgment. In the case described, Shane does not have hitting a bull's eye as an option. Hitting the bull's eye is not something that is in his power. To put the point another way, his control over the world is not sufficiently fine-grained for (7) to be true of him. So the present view explains why, on at least one reading, (7) is false.

Finally, the present view can capture the fact that there are two readings of (8):

(8) Sasha was able to hit the bull's eye

Recall that we are considering (8) relative to the case where Sasha is a mediocre darts player who has just now hit the bull's eye. We said that there is an equivocation on whether (8) is true or false. The present view can capture that equivocation. On the specific reading, (8) is true just in case Sasha had the option of hitting the bull's eye. Given that she has just hit the bull's eye, she had the option of hitting it—that follows from the Performance Principle. So there is a reading on which (8) is true, namely the specific reading. On the other hand, there is also a reading on which (8) is false. This is the *general* reading of 'able'-sentences.

3.7   'Able': The General Reading

Consider the reading on which the following is false:

(8) Sasha was able to hit the bull's eye

On this reading, merely having had a certain option on some occasion does not suffice for the truth of (8). What then does suffice for the truth of (8)?

I propose that, on its general reading, (8) involves an implicit *generic operator* GEN. The semantics of the generic operator are an ongoing subject of dispute, but the basic idea is familiar. Consider a sentence such as:

3 The Analysis of Ability   51

(9) Giraffes have spots

This sentence is true, but it does not demand either that every giraffe has spots—there may be, after all, exceptions. Nor does it suffice for (9) that exactly one giraffe has spots—that seems not to be enough. (9) is true because, at an intuitive level, giraffes *generally* have spots. The generic operator formalizes this intuitive observation.

If (8) involves a generic operator, over what is it is an operator? I propose that it is simply an operator over the options of the agent in question, so that the general reading is essentially generated from the specific reading through the implicit application of the generic operator.[5] That is, (8) is true, on its general reading, just in case Sasha generally has the option of hitting the bull's eye. But Sasha does not, generally, have this act as an option. She, like Shane, is a mediocre darts player, and a mediocre darts player does not generally have hitting the bull's eye as an option, or as something that is within her power. So, on its general reading, (8) is false.

More generally, consider some 'able'-sentence:

S is able to A

Where 'S' is a name denoting some agent S and 'A' is a phrase denoting some act α. I propose that, *on its general reading*, this sentence is true just in case:

GEN(S OPT α)

Let us now revisit the previous sentences we considered above and show what the present account says when each of these sentences is given its general reading.

It was argued, against the Ascription View, that, in the circumstances described above, (2) is false and (3) is true:

---

[5] Structurally, this account parallels Bhatt (1999), which is a crucial inspiration for the present account. Bhatt rejects both the Ascription View and the Modal View. He proposes a view on which 'able'-sentences have as their primary reading an implicative verb whose semantics are like that of 'manage to,' and a secondary reading in terms of a generic operator over that implicative verb. Bhatt's view, however, fails to accommodate the breadth of 'able'-sentences, especially those concerning acts that an agent will never (and would never) perform. In order to accommodate such sentences, we need to avail ourselves of a framework of options.

52   J. T. Maier

(2) Simone is able to speak French
(3) Sebastian is able to speak Japanese

The present view can accommodate the fact that these sentences are false and true, respectively: they are false and true, respectively, on their specific readings. But now it can also accommodate a sense in which (2) is true and (3) false. (2) is true on its general reading—Simone generally has speaking French as an option, for she generally is not under dental sedation. And (3) is false on its general reading—Sebastian does not generally have speaking Japanese as an option, for he generally does not have access to an automatic voice translator.

We can now somewhat complicate our objection to the Ascription View. The objection is not exactly that the Ascription View holds that (2) is true and (3) is false. As we have just said, the present view holds that (2) and (3) are, like (8), equivocal. Indeed, on the present view, any 'able'-sentence whatsoever has two readings, and as such is at least potentially equivocal. Rather, the objection more precisely is that the Ascription View cannot accommodate the sense in which (2) is false and (3) is true. Nor can it explain how that sense is related to another sense in which (2) is true and (3) is false. The present view, in contrast, gives a simple explanation of these phenomena. These are the specific and the general reading of these sentences, respectively, and the general is produced from the specific through the application of a generic operator.

The present view also explains—unlike the Modal View—why the truth of (4) does not ensure the truth of either (5) or (6):

(4) Sue is able to pick a red card or a black card
(5) Sue is able to pick a red card
(6) Sue is able to pick a black card

Earlier we argued that this implication (that is, from (4) to (5) or (6)) fails to hold on the specific reading of these sentences. Now we can argue that it also fails to hold on the general reading of these sentences. This implication pattern does not, in general, hold for generics. Consider:

(10) Playing cards are red or black
(11) Playing cards are red
(12) Playing cards are black

With respect to ordinary playing cards, (10) is true (the existence of exceptions, such as the Joker, does not invalidate the generic). Yet (11) and (12) are not true. Distribution over disjunction generally fails as a principle for generics.

Similarly, the truth of (4) implies the truth of neither (5) nor (6). Sue generally has the option of picking a red or a black card. But she does not generally have the option of picking a red card, and she does not generally have the option of picking a black card. As we said above, given her coarse-grained control over the world, neither one of these is generally within her power. So (5) and (6) are false. So the objectionable implication from (4) to (5) or (6), which appeared to be mandatory on the Modal View, fails on the present view on both the specific and the general reading of 'able'-sentences.

Finally, the present view, unlike the Modal View, holds that (7) is false:

(7) Shane is able to hit the bull's eye

Above I argued that (7) is false on its specific reading, since Shane does not have the option of hitting the bull's eye in the circumstances described. A fortiori, Shane does not generally have the option of hitting the bull's eye in the circumstances described. Thus (7) is false on its general as well as on its specific reading. Thus the present view holds that while (2), (3), and (8) are each true in one sense and false in another, (7) is unequivocally false in the circumstances described.

3.8 'Can'

I have now defended a systematic semantics for 'able'-sentences, on which these sentences involve *neither* the ascription of ability (as on the Ascription View) *nor* a modal operator (as on the Modal View). Instead, these sentences have a double aspect: on one reading, their specific reading, these sentences ascribe an option; on the other, their general reading, they involve a generic operator over options. This is an austere semantics that avails itself only of the generic operator and the underlying metaphysics of options articulated in the previous discussion.

I will presently turn from semantics back to metaphysics, and explain what this semantics of 'able'-sentences has to say about the project of giving a metaphysics for ability. Before coming to that, I want to consider another, related, semantic topic, as this is a worthy topic in its own right and one that further elucidates the subtle relationship between 'able'-sentences and modality.

When philosophers have attended to semantics considerations on agency and possibility, they have tended to take the modal auxiliary 'can' as their target.[6] 'Can' allegedly lies at the very root of philosophical perplexities about agency, and a correct semantics for 'can' has the potential to shed fresh light on those perplexities. But I want to suggest that 'can' is too coarse a target, for at least a couple of reasons.

First, whereas 'able' sentences apply most naturally to agents, or to things considered as agents,[7] 'can' sentences appear to be wider in their application. Thus while (13) is unproblematically true, (14) appears to involve a kind of presupposition failure:

(13) The rain can fall in Spain
(14) The rain is able to fall in Spain??

More formally, 'can' appears to take any possible verb phrase in its complement, whereas 'able' appears more restricted in its application, and the restriction appears to have something to do with agency.

Second, and relatedly, 'can' tolerates a null subject, whereas 'able' clearly does not. Thus (15) is clearly acceptable whereas (16) is clearly not:

---

[6] This philosophical-semantic tradition may reach its high-water mark in writings such as Austin (1956) and Taylor (1960), but it continues in contemporary work such as the aforementioned (Vetter, 2013).

[7] Since 'able'-sentences with non-agents as their subjects are sometimes true, the present semantics calls for an account of what it is for something to be 'considered as' an agent, and what it is to speak of an object as if it has options. As a first pass at such an account, I propose that to assert an 'able'-sentence about a non-agentive object is to take up what Dennett (1987) calls the 'intentional stance' towards that object. The metaphysical significance of the apparent attribution of abilities to mere objects will be taken up again, at greater length, in Chap. 4.

(15) It can get cold in Berlin
(16) It is able to get cold in Berlin*

This again suggests a connection to agency, since 'able,' being intimately connected to agency, demands a subject, whereas 'can,' whose connection to agency is perhaps more remote, does not.

These points suggest that the semantics I have proposed for 'able'-sentences cannot be extended to 'can'-sentences. The attribution of options to agents cannot be intelligibly understood as the foundation of the truth of (13) or (15). The recognition of this point about 'can' does not undermine the present semantics of 'able'-sentences. On the contrary, the present account is in a good position to explain why 'able'-sentences are restricted in their application, why that application is especially connected to agency, and why they have been a special focus of philosophical attention. All these facts are explained by the fact that the semantics of 'able'-sentences involve an appeal to agents' options.

The present semantics does not, then, purport to give a semantics for 'can.' It does however impose a significant constraint on any such semantics. Note that if (1) is true then (17) must also be true:

(1) Sam is able to build a bookshelf
(17) Sam can build a bookshelf

More generally, consider some 'able'-sentence:

S is able to A

Where 'S' is a name denoting some agent S and 'A' is a phrase denoting some act α. And consider some 'can'-sentence:

S can A

Where 'S' is a name denoting that same agent S and 'A' is a phrase denoting that same act α. Then, I propose, if that 'able'-sentence is true then the 'can'-sentence is true.

Note that this implication runs in only one direction. The opposite direction is rendered uncertain by pairs such as (13) and (14):

56   J. T. Maier

(13) The rain can fall in Spain
(14) The rain is able to fall in Spain??

The truth of (13) does not entail the truth of (14), for it is not clear that (14) even has a truth-value. The same point applies, even more strongly, to the pair (15) and (16):

(15) It can get cold in Berlin[8]
(16) It is able to get cold in Berlin*

In short, 'can'-sentences do not generally imply 'able'-sentences, because there is not always a corresponding 'able'-sentence for a given 'can'-sentences. In contrast, every 'able'-sentences implies a corresponding 'can'-sentence.

This implication pattern is something that a semantics of 'can' should explain. And, if the foregoing semantics of 'able'-sentences is correct, that semantics should turn on special features of options. Here is the kind of explanation that would satisfy that demand. Let us say that a modal view is true of 'can,' and specifically that a sentence of the form 'S can A' is to be understood in terms of existential quantification over possible worlds, as is argued in Kratzer (1981). Then the implication of (17) by (1)—and of 'can'-sentences by 'able'-sentences more generally—may be underwritten by, first, the specific reading of (1), and second, the Possibility Principle for options. The exact form of this explanation will depend on the details of the modal view in question, but this is the general form that such an explanation might take.

This explanation may nonetheless fail, for we have already encountered considerations against the modal view of 'can'-sentences. They are the very considerations that led us, above, to reject this kind of view of 'able'-sentences. So it may well be that we should adopt some different semantics of 'can'-sentences. The present argument takes no stand on what that semantics should look like. It simply demands that any such semantics

---

[8] See Portner (2009) for a thorough discussion of sentences such as (15) and the challenge that they seem to pose to standard semantic theories of 'can.'

should accommodate and ideally explain the fact that 'can'-sentences are implied by 'able'-sentences, and not conversely.

3.9 'Ability'

The nominal topic of our discussion is ability. But thus far I have focused on 'able'-sentences, and have given a systematic semantics for sentences such as:

(1) Sam is able to build a bookshelf

On the present semantics, 1 has a specific reading and a general reading, both of which are made true by facts about Sam's options.

We have not yet explicitly considered, however, sentences such as (18):

(18) Sam has the ability to build a bookshelf

One might reasonably propose that an account of the semantics of ability and its attribution should have something to say about (18).

I respond that the semantics of (18) have already been given. (18) effectively forces a general reading of (1), so that it is true just in case Sam generally has building a bookshelf as an option. More generally, consider some 'ability'-sentence:

S has the ability to A

Where 'S' is a name denoting some agent S and 'A' is a phrase denoting some act α. I propose that such a sentence is true just in case:

GEN(S OPT α)

The semantics of 'ability'-sentences is simply then a special case of the more general semantics for 'able'-sentences.

This view of 'ability'-sentences elegantly captures our judgments in cases where the truth of certain 'able'-sentences diverges from corresponding 'ability'-sentences. This is precisely what happened in the case of those sentences that posed difficulties for the Ascription View. Consider again:

(2) Simone is able to speak French

Above I argued that the Ascription View of (2) cannot be correct, as (2) is false in the circumstances described (temporary sedation) even though Simone retains the ability to speak French in those circumstances. Thus (2) cannot be an ascription to Simone of the ability to speak French.

We are now in a position to restate this view more formally. The case described shows that the Ascription View cannot capture the specific reading of (2). However, there is a nearby sentence that admits only of a general reading, and this sentence remains true in the circumstances described:

(19) Simone has the ability to speak French

The Ascription View gets the truth-value of (19) correct, but it gets that of (2) incorrect. The present view, in contrast, captures the equivocal status of (2) and derives (19) as a special case where only the general reading is available. It thereby yields the more parsimonious account of both 'able'-sentences and 'ability'-sentences, and the relationship between the two.

This semantic theory of 'ability'-sentences also coheres nicely with their apparent morphology. 'Ability' is a nominalization of the modal adjective 'able.' While we should not generally expect the semantics of a nominalization to be derivable from the semantics of its base form (Chomsky, 1970), in this case there is in fact a close connection: the semantics of 'ability'-sentences simply correspond to one reading of 'able'-sentences. Thus, a semantics for 'ability'-sentences is effectively already implicit in a semantics for 'able'-sentences.

We thus arrive at a view that is semantically and methodologically almost the inverse of the Ascription View. The Ascription View posits things such as abilities and takes sentences such as (1) and (18) to ascribe them. The present view posits no such thing. Rather, it gives a semantics for a modal adjective 'able' in terms of a metaphysics of options (along with the generic operator). Insofar as it introduces abilities, it does so only as nominalizations of this underlying adjective. We might say that on the present view abilities are only mentioned, and never used. The remainder of the discussion draws out the metaphysical implications of this observation.

3.10 A Theory of Ability

Near the outset of this chapter, we asked the following questions: what is it for an agent to have an ability? That is, what is it for some agent to be able to do something—for instance, to be able to build a house? We are now in a position to answer these questions.

To begin, let us consider some particular ability, such as Sam's ability to build a bookshelf. We will give an account of this ability in three steps.

First, note that Sam has the ability to build a bookshelf if and only if the sentence (18) is true:

(18) Sam has the ability to build a bookshelf

This first step follows from a trivial principle of disquotation: that something is the case if and only if the sentence expressing that it is the case is true.

Second, as has been argued in this chapter, (18) is true if and only if Sam generally has the option of building a bookshelf, where 'generally' is to be understood in terms of the generic operator GEN. This is a semantic claim about the truth-conditions of a sentence, and as such makes no claim about the metaphysics of ability per se. It is simply a claim about the correct semantics of a certain natural language construction, a semantics that has been defended at length in the foregoing.

From these two steps it follows that Sam has the ability to build a bookshelf just in case Sam generally has the option of building a bookshelf. The third and last step is the metaphysical one. Once we note that we have given a full account of the semantics of (18) without quantifying over abilities, we can see that our ordinary claims about abilities do not in fact commit us to abilities. We may then say, not only that Sam's ability is correlated with certain options, but that what it is for Sam to have that ability simply is for Sam to have options of a certain sort. So, third, we claim that what it is for Sam to have an ability to build a bookshelf is for Sam to generally have the option of building a bookshelf. Whereas our earlier claims were symmetric, this is an asymmetric claim of dependence: Sam's ability to build a bookshelf depends on Sam's options, and not conversely.

60   J. T. Maier

More generally, consider some claim of the form: S has the ability to A, where 'S' is a name denoting some agent S and 'A' is a phrase denoting some act α. I propose that what it is for such a claim to hold—that is, what it is for a given agent to have a given ability—is for the following formula to be true:

GEN(S OPT α)

To put this formal claim in somewhat more picturesque language, the proposal is that there is nothing to abilities but patterns in the space of options. If some agent generally has some act as an option, then she has the ability to act in that way—for that is simply what it is to have an ability.

3.11   Are There Abilities?

When we initially considered the question of what it is to have an ability, we considered the Megarian view of ability described by Aristotle: '*There are some, e.g. the Megaric school, who say that a thing only has potency when it functions.*' One way of thinking of the Megarian view is as an error theory of ability (or of 'potency'): since a being has an ability only when it acts, there are really no such things as abilities, at least as we ordinarily conceive them. This may be the aspect of the view that led Aristotle to say that it had 'absurd consequences.' While the present view is not Megarian, one might argue that it too holds that it too is a kind of error theory that holds that, really, there are no such things as abilities, and that it too has absurd consequences.

Are there abilities, on the present view? The ontological consequences of a theory are not always easy to ascertain. We might say that a theory accepts that there are abilities if and only if it accepts the truth of sentences that say that there are abilities. On this very weak sense, the present view certainly does accept that there are abilities, for it accepts that sentences such as (18) may be true:

(18) Sam has the ability to build a bookshelf

However, this is a very weak standard, as in this sense most of us accept the existence of 'nobodies,' since we accept that the following sentence may be true

(20) Sam has nobody to take to the party

This superficial linguistic test for existence, then, is too liberal to credit.

A somewhat more demanding view holds that something exists if there is a true sentence whose correct semantics quantifies over that thing. On this more stringent condition, the truth of (18) does not commit us to the existence of (18) since, as I have just argued, the correct semantics for (18) does not quantify over abilities. The truth of (18) no more requires the existence of abilities than the truth of (20) requires the existence of 'nobodies.'

Are there abilities? The present view answers this question with some care. Our ordinary thought and talk about abilities is true on its own terms. But this discourse does not quantify over abilities, in the same way that (for example) our ordinary thought and talk about tables quantifies over tables. The 'metaphysics of ability,' insofar as there is such a thing, will be a linguistically mediated enterprise, insofar as abilities do not have an independent claim to our attention, but are simply a shadow cast by our ways of speaking about our options.

3.12 Specific and General Abilities

This proposal solves, or dissolves, certain perplexities in the theory of ability.

Consider the distinction between specific and general abilities. This distinction is taken as axiomatic in certain standard treatments of ability. It is usually introduced by way of example:

> Consider a well-trained tennis player equipped with ball and racquet, standing at the service line. There is, as it were, nothing standing between her and a serve: every prerequisite for her serving has been met ... Let us say that such an agent has the specific ability to serve. In contrast, consider an otherwise similar

tennis player who lacks a racquet and ball, and is miles away from a tennis court. There is clearly a good sense in which such an agent has the ability to hit a serve: she has been trained to do so, and has done so many times in the past. Yet such an agent lacks the specific ability to serve, as that term was just defined. Let us say that such an agent has the general ability to serve. (Maier, 2020)

This purportedly intuitive distinction raises as many questions as it answers. What are these two kinds of ability? Are they two metaphysically distinct phenomena, or two modes of a single phenomenon? Is one prior to the other, and if so how? And why are there exactly two kinds of ability—why not one, or three, or for that matter an infinite number?

The present view gives answers to all these questions. The distinction between specific and general ability is a legitimate one, but its grounds are ultimately linguistic in origin. It reflects the fact that there is a generic operator permitted in ability ascriptions. There are exactly two kinds of ability because there is exactly one operator, which may either be present or absent. General ability corresponds to the presence of the general operator. Specific ability corresponds to its absence.

The metaphysical questions posed about specific ability and general ability are dealt with in a similar fashion. Talking as if there are two kinds of ability is something of a misleading reification of a fundamentally linguistic distinction—but then, so too 's speaking of ability in the first place. Finally, to the question of which of specific and general ability is more fundamental than the other, the present account answers that neither is more fundamental than the other, any more than the general reading of 'able'-sentences is more or less fundamental than their specific readings.

In another sense, however, it is the specific ability that is more fundamental. For specific ability may be thought of, ultimately, as just another name for options. And it is options that are, on the present view, fundamental. Insofar as there is something that lies underneath this distinction in ability, and indeed underwrites our thought and talk of ability, it is agents and their options.

3 The Analysis of Ability   63

3.13   Abilities Regained?

I have argued that the truth of our ordinary thought and talk about abilities does not require the existence of abilities, any more than the truth of our ordinary thought and talk about nobodies requires the existence of nobodies. Claims about abilities are perfectly legitimate on their own terms, but the quantification that occurs to them is to be understood superficially. Abilities are a linguistic device for speaking of what is fundamental in the theory of agency, namely options.

Someone might protest that, even if the semantic proposals defended in this chapter are correct, there might yet be other reasons to accept that there are abilities. After all, there are things whose existence we accept because they are posits of some theory we accept: electrons, for instance. The canonical criterion for existence is not what is quantified over in the true sentences of a natural language—which is the criterion I have been focusing on thus far—but what is quantified over in the theory that best explains the phenomena as we encounter them. And it may well be that abilities satisfy this somewhat more refined ontological criterion.

Do abilities figure in explanations? We certainly do sometimes give explanations that appeal to abilities. Sam builds a bookshelf. We ask for an explanation for how she did this. One explanation we might give, in certain contexts, is that she had the ability to build the bookshelf. For instance, if another person Sal had the same equipment and materials as Sam, and yet failed to build a bookshelf, we might well cite Sam's ability to build a bookshelf in explaining why she succeeded where Sal failed.

This kind of appeal to ability, however, is altogether compatible with the view of ability endorse here. To appeal to Sam's ability is to appeal to the fact that she generally has certain options. And that fact in turn will itself have a further explanation—one that appeals to Sam's physiology and psychology, and perhaps also to certain environmental factors. None of this is incompatible with a view on which abilities are, as on the present view, a linguistically mediated construction.

On the present view, our appeals to abilities in explanation are not unlike the appeal to the 'dormitive virtues' of opium. This is not to say that these are bad explanations. To say that opium puts people to sleep because of its dormitive virtues is to convey, in a concise and informative way, that opium has the effect it does largely because of internal features of the drug (see Lewis (1986)). In the same way, to say that Sam built the bookshelf because she had the ability to do so is to attribute her success largely to Sam, rather than to external factors. But the appeal to abilities here is simply a convenient shorthand. As our theory of the physiological effects of opium can dispense with an appeal to its dormitive virtues, so can our theory of agency dispense with an appeal to abilities.

The foregoing argument does not rule out all arguments for including abilities in our ontology. I have in mind, specifically, empirical arguments for abilities. Several psychological theories, that at least purport to be explanatory, make reference to abilities or to ability-like notions. Consider intelligence. Many psychologists and other social scientists appeal to something like intelligence and invoke it to explain, for example, differential educational outcomes. The arguments for the existence of such an ability are in fact subject to serious challenges (such as Gould (1996)) and the framework developed here may well lend semantic and metaphysical support to those challenges. I do not however mean to be offering an a priori argument that there could be no abilities. The conclusions of this discussion, with respect to ontology, are more modest.

First, the deliverances of common sense and of ordinary discourse are of no support whatsoever for taking seriously an ontology of abilities. We do often make claims about agents' abilities, and when we do, we speak truly, but such claims do not really quantify over abilities. This is an illusion of nominalization. Really, what makes true claims about abilities are generic facts about agents' options. In this sense, talk of abilities is a convenient shorthand for talk about options.

Second, abilities are not indispensable to the theory of agency, as they can sometimes seem to be. We can give a simple account of agents, and of what they are able to do, without any appeal to abilities at all. We may instead appeal to options. In this sense, there is simply no need for the hypothesis of abilities to give an explanatory account of agency and possibility of the kind being developed here.

Bibliography

Austin, J. L. (1956). Ifs and Cans. *Proceedings of the British Academy, 42*, 109–132.

Bhatt, R. (1999). *Covert Modality in Non-Finite Contexts.* Dissertation, University of Pennsylvania.

Chomsky, N. (1970). Remarks on Nominalization. In R. A. Jacobs & P. S. Rosenbaum (Eds.), *Readings in English Transformational Grammar.* Ginn and Company.

Dennett, D. C. (1987). *The Intentional Stance.* MIT Press.

Gould, S. J. (1996). *The Mismeasure of Man.* W. W. Norton & Company.

Kratzer, A. (1981). The Notional Category of Modality. In H. J. Eikmeyer & H. Rieser (Eds.), *Words, Worlds, and Contexts.* De Gruyter.

Lewis, D. K. (1986). Causal Explanation. In *Philosophical Papers Vol. II.* Oxford University Press.

Maier, J. (2020). Abilities. In *The Stanford Encyclopedia of Philosophy* (E.N. Zalta, Ed.). Metaphysics Research Lab, Stanford University.

Makin, S. (2006). *Aristotle: Metaphysics Theta.* Oxford University Press.

Mandelkern, M., Schultheis, G., & Boylan, D. (2017). Agentive Modals. *Philosophical Review, 126*(3), 301–343.

Taylor, R. (1960). I Can. *Philosophical Review, 69*(1), 78–89.

Vetter, B. (2013). 'Can' Without Possible Worlds: Semantics for Anti-Humeans. *Philosophers' Imprint, 13.*

4

The Active and Passive Powers

4.1 Agency and Analysis

The methodology of the discussion to this point has been resolute in taking agency first. I have aimed to understand agentive modality and ability and their own terms, and not by the lights of some more general theory initially developed to capture non-agents, and then extended to the agentive case. I have insisted, on the contrary, on a theoretically bespoke approach to agency.

As I have noted at various points, most authors have proceeded differently. The orthodox approach to agency in the recent philosophical tradition has been to take a broad philosophical approach and give an account of particular agentive phenomena in terms of it. My view is that such approaches will almost always be inadequate, not because I think there is a proof that this kind of methodology is bound to fail but because the history of such attempts is a series of unconvincing proposals. There are in fact two ways in which these kinds of proposals may fail that can be distinguished.

First, the proposal might simply not do justice to the phenomena. For instance, as was argued in the foregoing, an approach to the semantics of

© The Author(s), under exclusive license to Springer Nature Switzerland AG 2022   **67**
J. T. Maier, *Options and Agency*, https://doi.org/10.1007/978-3-031-10243-1_4

68   J. T. Maier

agentive modality in terms of standard modal logic simply does not do justice to the implications that are valid, and that are not valid, for agentive notions like that of an option. The objections to accounts of agency that I have made in the foregoing have all pointed to failures of this first kind.

The second kind of failure is more subtle. It might be that these proposals are circular in the following sense. It may be that the very notions that are being used to analyze agentive ones ultimately depend on agency. So these proposals fail as explanatory accounts, even if they are extensionally adequate. We have not yet encountered an example of this second kind, but in the following I give a sustained objection with precisely this shape. This second kind of analytic failure is the more serious of the two, because it cannot be resolved merely by modifying the proposed account. It shows that the entire approach is mistaken.

This second kind of failure, however, also points to a positive project. While the analysis of an agentive notion in terms of something non-agentive fails, and fundamentally so, a different possibility becomes apparent: analyzing the purportedly non-agentive notion in wholly agentive terms. These kinds of analyses have generally been outside the ken of mainstream philosophy,[1] but, as I will argue here, they have much to commend them, for agency is a pervasive feature of our world, even when it is not recognized as such.

It will be helpful to move from these broader methodological considerations to consider a specific analysis and its shortcomings.

4.2   The Dispositional Analysis of Ability

In the foregoing I have considered and rejected the idea that ability is to be analyzed in some sense in terms of power. Rather, ability is to be understood in terms of agents' options. I want to return however to the idea that ability should be analyzed in terms of powers, and to one

---

[1] A notable exception are attempts to analyze causation in agentive terms, of the kind defended in Menzies and Price (1993).

4 The Active and Passive Powers   69

manifestation of that idea that has enjoyed some currency in the recent philosophical literature.

This proposal begins with the idea of a disposition. As I will presently argue, it is not entirely clear what counts as a disposition, but the fragility of a glass is often cited as a canonical example. A fragile glass is disposed to break when struck. Of particular interest is that dispositionality feels somehow related to possibility, as dispositions may exist even when they are not manifested. A glass remains fragile even when it does not break, and even when put in circumstances where it is not easily broken.

Several authors have noticed that, in this respect and others, abilities are rather like dispositions.[2] Consider someone's ability to speak French. Like a glass's fragility, this is something that can exist even when unmanifested. Someone who has the ability to speak French retains it even when she is not speaking French, and indeed even when speaking French is, for one reason or another, not an available act in the circumstances.[3] In these respects, an ability behaves much like a disposition. This suggests that it is simply is a disposition of some kind.

To develop this suggestion, we need to answer the following question. A disposition is a disposition to manifest some activity when given a certain kind of stimulus. For instance, fragility is at first approximation a disposition to break (the manifestation) when struck (the stimulus). What then are the manifestation and stimulus for an ability?[4] The manifestation seems clear enough: it is the action in question. To manifest the ability to speak French is simply to speak French. But what is the stimulus?

This question is standardly answered in a familiar way. The stimulus for an ability is some act of will, such as a choice, an intention, or a trying. This is an old idea from the conditional analysis of options, now figuring instead as an element in the dispositional analysis of ability. We will return to the question of whether the new proposal simply revives the

---

[2] See Smith (2003), Vihvelin (2004), and Fara (2008); see also Clarke (2009) for a critical overview.
[3] This is simply an instance of a point already emphasized, namely that an agent may retain the ability to perform an act even at times when that act is not an option.
[4] A different approach would be to allow for dispositions to lack stimulus conditions, and to model abilities on dispositions that are monadic in this way. Although Fara (2005) endorses precisely this possibility in the case of dispositions, it is not one that he or other advocates of a dispositional analysis pursue in their accounts of ability.

problems of the old one. Postponing that issue for now, and putting the pieces together, we arrive at the following analysis:

(DA)   S has the ability to A just in case S is disposed to A when S chooses to A

An agent has the ability to speak French, for instance, just in case she is disposed to speak French when she chooses to. This is plausibly a disposition that a native French speaker has and that someone unfamiliar with the French language lacks. Further, and crucially, this is not offered merely as an observation about abilities and dispositions but as a reduction of the one to the other. What it is to have the ability to speak French is simply to have a disposition of a certain sort. There is no further problem about what abilities are.

One can raise further questions about the proposal DA. Notably, it is a vexed question what dispositions themselves are, and one wants an account of dispositions for this analysis to be fully informative. And this is a point, I will shortly argue, on which this analysis of ability founders.

4.3   First Argument Against Dispositionalism

I noted above that approaches to the analysis of agentive notions can fail in two ways: by failing to be extensionally adequate, or by covertly presupposing agentive notions. Let us begin with objections of the first kind to what I will call 'dispositionalism'—that is, to the dispositional analysis of ability and specifically to the proposal DA.

These objections are ones that we have already encountered, under another guise, as objections to the conditional analysis of options. The dispositional analysis differs in its analysans and its analysandum. It is an analysis of abilities, not options. And it appeals to dispositions, not counterfactual conditionals, in its analysis. Nonetheless, it has a structural similarity to the conditional analysis: it offers a two-place analysis of a superficially monadic agentive modality, analyzing it in terms of a modal relation between the agent's volition and her actions. This structural aspect of the dispositional analysis makes it subject to objections much like those that created trouble for the conditional analysis of options.

4 The Active and Passive Powers   71

In the discussion of the conditional analysis, I offered three distinct objections: cases of psychological compulsion, Frankfurt cases, and cases of the absence of volition. There is extensive discussion in the literature on the dispositional analysis as to whether cases of the first and second kind in fact tell against the dispositional analysis.[5] These discussions hang on rather fine intuitions about ability claims in unusual circumstances. (On the view of ability that I defended in Chap. 3, it is to be expected that our judgments in these cases will be uncertain, as generics do not always set a sharp context-independent threshold for when they do or do not obtain. In this respect they are different from options, which do allow for this kind of sharpness of judgment.) I propose therefore to set aside these cases and focus on the third objection leveled in the early discussion.

This objection, recall, was that agents could be subjects of agentive modality even if they simply did not have any volitions. This objection is, if anything, more compelling in the case of abilities than it is in the case of options. Consider especially the case of non-human animals. Consider a simple animal that can navigate its environment, consume energy, mate, and so forth. But imagine that, for such an agent, there is no mental state that deserves the name volition. This agent simply acts in a way that maximizes its well-being or other parameters, without that act being mediated by any mental representation. I wish to defend two claims about such an agent: that it is possible, and that it has abilities.

The first of these claims follows from basic combinatorial principles. As behavior and mental representation are distinct aspects of agency, we can have one of these without the other in the way described. It might be that there is an account of the metaphysics of agency on which this is not in fact a live possibility, and that might be a premise in a larger defense of the dispositional analysis, but I am not aware of any such account. Absent such an account, our default position should be that such an animal is possible, and for all we know many even be actual.[6]

The second of these claims follows simply for our judgments about the conditions under which agents have abilities. An agent that navigates its

---

[5] See again Clarke (2009) for a careful adjudication of these responses and whether they succeed.
[6] For a discussion of some of the open empirical debates that bear on this question, see Dickinson (2011).

environment in this way at least appears to be an agent with abilities. We might insist that such an agent does not have abilities, but it is difficult to see what theory of agency might underwrite that insistence. Animal agency, I want to suggest, is agency that involves abilities, whether or not the more sophisticated psychological demands imposed by the dispositional analysis are met.

The case of non-human agents is not considered by advocates of the dispositional analysis. The diagnosis of this shortcoming is the same as in the case of the conditional analysis of options. In that case, I argued that what advocates of the conditional analysis were really providing was an account of something like autonomous agency, of an agent whose acts depend in the proper way on her volitions. I want to suggest that advocates of the dispositional analysis are doing something similar. An agent who is disposed to do what she chooses to do will be one who can generally stick to her resolutions, both across time and across nearby possibilities. This kind of resolution is an important virtue for an agent to have, considering the variability of incentives and the downsides of deviating from one's plans.[7] And it is plausible that having this virtue is a matter of having certain dispositions. So the dispositional analysis may well capture an important aspect of well-governed agency. It simply does not constitute an adequate account of ability.[8]

4.4   What Is a Disposition?

There remains a more foundational question to be asked about the dispositional analysis: does the notion of a disposition itself presuppose some agentive notions? If it does, then the consequences of this ramify well beyond the present topic. Dispositions have figured as an unexplained explainer in philosophical accounts of the mind, of the secondary

---

[7] On the distinctive roles of resolution, see Holton (2004).

[8] As I have already argued in Chap. 3, we should in the end be skeptical of the idea that there is even such a thing as ability, properly speaking. An account of ability should be replaced by an account of 'able'-sentences, which gives an account of their truth conditions without any appeal to abilities at all. But the objections brought against dispositionalism here arise even granting the assumption that there are such things as abilities.

4 The Active and Passive Powers 73

qualities, of value, and much else. If dispositions are covertly agentive, then so too may be many other aspects of the world as we find it.

It is therefore important to ask: what is a disposition? This question admits of at least two readings. First, it may ask for an analysis of dispositions, an account of what it is to have a disposition told in non-dispositional terms. This is the reading of the question that has been foregrounded in most philosophical discussions. I will ultimately consider this question, but I want to begin by focusing on a second reading. On this reading, the question asks for a principle of demarcation: what is it that distinguishes paradigmatically dispositional properties, such as fragility, from the various properties that do not appear to be dispositional. This question does not ask for an analysis—though that might be one way in which to answer it—but simply to fix the scope of what demands an analysis in the first place.

The class of dispositions is often defined by ostension: being fragile is a disposition, and so too are being flammable and being irascible.[9] In the absence of any metaphysical principle to guide us, we might begin by asking a linguistic question. What is it about these predicates that makes them dispositional? This question has a semantic reading, on which its answer is clear: what makes these predicates dispositional is that they denote dispositions. That answer is clear, but uninformative: it gets us no closer to an account of how to distinguish dispositions from non-dispositions.

An alternative way is to proceed morphologically. Dispositional predicates generally are characterized by the use of the '-ble' suffix.[10] Furthermore, this morphological aspect of dispositional predicates is not accidental, but seems to be closely connected to their semantics, and particularly to certain 'able'-sentences. At first approximation, a flammable blanket is one that is easily able to be burned, and an irascible person is someone who is easily able to be angered. This suggests that the morpho-

---

[9] In the contemporary literature on dispositions, authors often appeal to locutions such as 'The glass is disposed to break when struck' in lieu of predicates like those used in the text. See Maier (2015) for a discussion of these locutions and how they are related to the dispositional predicates that are more common in ordinary speech and that will be the focus here.

[10] Sometimes historical phonetic pressures will lead to the modification of this suffix, for example in 'fragile' which takes an '-le' suffix.

logical marker of dispositional predicates does have a deeper semantic significance.

Once this point is recognized, however, it appears to generalize dramatically. For there are many predicates that involve '-ble' predicates that are not typically characterized as dispositions. Consider being walkable or being lovable. Each of these seems constitutively connected to an 'able'-sentence. A walkable trail is one that is easily able to be walked. A lovable person is one who is easily able to be loved. Yet, unlike flammability and irascibility, walkability and lovability are not typically characterized as dispositions. Why not?

To begin to answer that question, it is helpful to ask how we do characterize properties such as walkability and lovability. An apt label for these kinds of properties is James J. Gibson's notion of an affordance: 'The affordances of the environment are what it offers the animal, what it provides or furnishes, either for good or ill' (Gibson, 1979).[11] The walkability of a trail is a paradigmatic affordance: a walkable trail makes the possibility of walking available. So too is the lovability of a person: a lovable person makes the possibility of love available.[12] There appears to be an internal connection between affordances and the '-ble' suffix, such that the combination of an arbitrary verb phrase with '-ble' typically generates an affordance-predicate, a linguistic device often deployed by Gibson. Thus, if a particular rock is easy to pick up, we might aptly describe it as pick-up-able, and our meaning is readily understood.

In light of that observation, we can slightly revise our question. Our question was: why are walkability and lovability not counted as dispositions? We might now instead ask: why are flammability and irascibility counted as dispositions? After all, the default case seems to be for the '-ble' suffix to generate an affordance. Why, in these special cases, does it instead generate a disposition?

---

[11] Compare Goodman (1955), who famously introduces the topic of dispositions as follows: 'Besides the observable properties it exhibits and the actual processes it undergoes, a thing is full of threats and promises' (p. 40). This language suggests a thesis that I will elaborate in what follows: that Gibson and Goodman are approaching, by different routes and under different names, something like a single phenomenon.

[12] On the extension of affordances to the interpersonal case, see Brancazio (2020).

4 The Active and Passive Powers 75

I want to suggest that there is a relatively simple linguistic explanation for this phenomenon. Flammable is associated with the verb burn, and irascible is associated with the verb anger. These verbs are notable because they allow a certain transition from the passive to the active voice. If a blanket is burned, then it burns. If a person is angered, then she angers. And, to return to the case of fragility, if a glass is broken, it breaks. These verbs display what we can call *pseudo-activity*: they attribute to an object an action that is in fact the action of an external agent who is acting on that object.[13]

We can now return to our question of demarcation: what distinguishes dispositional properties from non-dispositional properties? Our first step is to move from the material to the formal mode, and ask: what distinguishes dispositional predicates from non-dispositional predicates? Dispositional predicates may be thought of as a species of a genus, which is those predicates that are formed from '-ble' predicates. In the default case, these predicates designate affordances, in Gibson's sense of that term, such as being walkable, being lovable, and being pick-up-able. But in the special case where they involve verbs that allow for pseudo-activity (such as burn, break, and anger), these predicates form the class of '-ble' predicates that have come to be recognized as dispositional ones.

Having answered the demarcation question, we can return to the analytic one. What is it to have a disposition? And what, if anything, is the significance of being a disposition as opposed to simply being an affordance?

4.5   A Theory of Dispositions

In terms of the foregoing, we can give an account of what dispositions are: that is, an account in non-dispositional terms of what it is for something to have a disposition.

---

[13] Pseudo-activity corresponds to what Maier (2015) calls 'ergativity.' Following the approach developed there, we can give a formal criterion for pseudo-activity as follows. A verb V is pseudo-active just in case 'S V's x' implies 'x V's.' For instance, 'Sam breaks the glass' implies 'The glass breaks,' whereas 'Sam paints the glass' does not imply 'The glass paints.'

76   J. T. Maier

The theory proceeds in two steps. The first step is a kind of semantic ascent: a disposition is a property designated by a dispositional predicate. This move is underwritten by an observation already made, namely that the scope of dispositions appears to be shaped by the language in which we speak of them. It also yields a tractable object for philosophical analysis: the problem of giving an account of dispositions reduces to the problem of giving a morphology and semantics for dispositional predicates.

The second step is the following:

(DP)   F is a dispositional predicate just in case:
(i)   'F' is semantically associated with some verb V
(ii)   V is a pseudo-agentive verb
(iii) 'x is F' is true just in case x is easily able to be Ved

Let us go through the steps of DP for a paradigmatic dispositional predicate such as 'flammable.' First, 'flammable' is semantically associated with the verb 'burn.'[14] Second, as we have already argued, 'burn' is pseudo-agentive.[15] Third, and finally, something is flammable just in case it is easily able to be burned, a platitude we have already noted.[16] 'Flammable' is therefore a dispositional predicate. And, returning now to our first step, it follows that flammability is a disposition.

That is what it is for an object to have a disposition. Consider again our other question: what is the significance of having a disposition as opposed to having an affordance? To begin, let us give an account of affordances. The first step, as before, is to observe that a property is an affordance just in case it is denoted by an affordance predicate. The second step is to give an account of affordance predicates, as follows:

(AP)   F is affordance predicate just in case:
(i)   'F' is semantically associated with some verb phrase V
(ii)   'x is F' is true just in case x is easily able to be Ved

---

[14] A predicate is semantically associated with a verb, I will say, just in case the truth-conditions for the applicability of that predicate are best stated in terms of that verb. For instance, the best statement of the conditions under which an object is flammable will invoke the verb 'burn.'

[15] Invoking again our formal criterion, 'burn' is pseudo-agentive because 'Sam burns the blanket' implies 'The blanket burns.'

[16] On the close connection between dispositions and 'easily,' see Vetter (2014).

4 The Active and Passive Powers   77

There are two differences between AP and VP. First, AP allows for verb phrases generally and does not demand that the verb already be in the lexicon. This allows for the generation of neologistic predicates such as 'pick-up-able.' Second, AP does not demand that the predicate be generated from a pseudo-agentive verb.[17] Aside from these differences, however, the accounts are fundamentally similar.

We can stay still more. Not only are dispositional predicates and affordance predicates fundamentally similar, but the former are in some sense a special case of the latter. Dispositional predicates happen to have certain linguistic features—notably a pseudo-agentive aspect which involves the attribution of agency to their objects—but their semantics are fundamentally the same as affordance predicates. And, since on the present account there is nothing more to being a disposition or affordance than being denoted by a dispositional predicate or an affordance predicate, respectively, we can say that dispositions are a special case of affordances. And, since what distinguishes them is not any metaphysical feature but simply an aspect of their associated predicates, we can say that dispositions simply are affordances.

This perspective is altogether different from the one suggested by most recent work in analytic metaphysics. In that tradition, dispositions are regarded as a central feature of the world, and affordances as a far more marginal one. Indeed, some authors who have attempted to explain and legitimate the topic of affordances have proposed to do so by adopting standard views of dispositions and then analyzing affordances as a kind of disposition, so conceived (Scarantino, 2003). As just suggested, this has things exactly the wrong way around. It is affordances that constitute the more general class, while dispositions simply represent one restriction on that class.

There is another, older, metaphysical tradition within which the present view of dispositions is naturally understood. In this tradition, the

---

[17] If we wished, we could add a third condition that specifically demanded that the predicate not be semantically associated with a pseudo-agentive verb. That condition would construe affordances more narrowly, in accord with common usage, and would exclude—by fiat—properties like fragility from the class of affordances. I prefer the broader and more principled account given in the text, as it recognizes dispositions as a special case of affordances.

fundamental distinction is between active and passive powers.[18] An active power is the power to act, such as an animal's power to walk. A passive power is the power to be acted on, such as a trail's power to be walked on. It is difficult to fit the notion of a disposition, which seems to intermingle notions of both activity and passivity, into this traditional taxonomy. This is perhaps one reason why it has fallen out of favor.

Yet, on the present approach, this taxonomy is an illuminating one. For it offers us a clear way of understanding what dispositions are, as well as what distinguishes them from affordances generally. Dispositions, on the present view, are passive powers. This is why the key semantic condition in the analysis of dispositional predicates is put in the passive voice. To be flammable, for instance, is fundamentally to be something that is able to be burned. What distinguishes dispositions from affordances more generally is that they can be described as active powers, due to the linguistic device of pseudo-activity. Thus a flammable blanket, one that is able to be burned, can be described as one that has the power to burn. In contrast, a simple affordance such as walkability can only be described in passive terms. The language of active and passive power then yields a simple way of describing the present view of dispositions: dispositions are those properties that appear to be active powers but are really passive powers.

4.6 Finks and Masks

The philosophical literature on dispositions has been occupied with a curious set of questions: whether dispositional ascriptions are analyzable in terms of counterfactuals, and whether certain esoteric cases—cases of 'finks' and 'masks'—show that such an analysis fails. I want to briefly address these cases, not so much for their own sake as to approach the

---

[18] A locus classicus for this distinction, in the early modern tradition, is the following passage from Locke: *Thus we say, Fire has a power to melt gold, i.e. to destroy the consistency of its insensible parts, and consequently its hardness, and make it fluid; and gold has a power to be melted; that the sun has a power to blanch wax, and wax a power to be blanched by the sun ... Power thus considered is two-fold, viz. as able to make, or able to receive any change. The one may be called active, and the other passive power.* (Locke, 1690/1996)

4 The Active and Passive Powers 79

present approach to dispositions to the ones that have been more prominent in the recent literature.

Here, briefly described, is a case of finking and how it tells against the counterfactual analysis of dispositions.[19] Consider a thin glass vase. This vase is fragile, or disposed to break when struck. According to the conditional analysis of dispositions, this is true just in case the following counterfactual is true: if this vase were struck, it would break. That counterfactual does seem true in the ordinary case. Imagine however that there is a device attached to this vase, that will turn it from glass to steel if it is about to be struck. Given the presence of this device, the counterfactual is not true: if this vase were struck, it would not break. Nonetheless, the vase is actually fragile. So the conditional analysis of dispositions is to be rejected.

Consider now how this question looks when approached from a more affordance-centric point of view. From this point of view, we begin with the following question: can the vase be easily broken? Our answer to this question is, initially, equivocal. On the one hand, it is a thin glass vase, and these are easy to break, other things being equal. On the other, it has a finking device attached to it, and, when activated, that induces changes that make it extremely difficult to break. The question of whether a vase like this is easily broken is a vexed one, and not one normally encountered in our practical encounters with the world.

The best way forward on this question is, on the present view, a pragmatic one. The question of whether this particular glass is fragile will hang on questions that generally go undiscussed in the literature on these topics.[20] Is the finking device a permanent feature of the device, or is it one that is easily able to be removed? What would it take to remove it or to in some other way block its effects? As these details are not generally specified in discussions of finking, the question of whether a vase like this is fragile is simply indeterminate: it is not clearly fragile, and it is not clearly not fragile either.

---

[19] Such cases are due to Martin (1994). Strictly speaking, in Martin's nomenclature, the following case is a case of 'reverse finking.'

[20] An exception is Fara (2005), and his distinction between 'entrenched' and 'transient' finkishness.

80   J. T. Maier

Cases of masking are somewhat different. Consider again a thin glass vase. According to the conditional analysis of dispositions, as before, this vase is fragile just in case the following counterfactual is true: if the vase were struck, it would break. Now imagine the vase is filled, as such vases often are, with packing materials such as newspapers or styrofoam. Then, if this vase were struck, it would not break. The packing material prevents or 'masks' its breaking. Nonetheless, the vase is, in fact fragile. So the conditional analysis of dispositions again appears to fail.

There are two specific aspects in which cases of masking are different from cases of finking. First, these cases do not involve any intrinsic change to their objects. The vase remains just as it is, it simply is put in certain circumstances (namely, being filled with packing material). Second, while cases of finking exist primarily in the philosophical imagination, cases of masking are utterly common: vases are packed with packing material, flammable blankets are sprayed with flame-retardant liquid, and irascible people are given calming medications. As we live in a world of dispositions with unfortunate outcomes, and as masking tends to be a simple and cost-effective way of preventing these outcomes, we live also in a world of masks.

From the pragmatic point of view suggested by the present view of dispositions, this second difference is the crucial one. As masks are common, we have some familiarity with them and the ways in which they may be removed or undone, and this familiarity underwrites our judgments about them. A glass vase filled with packing material is fragile, according to the present account. Why? Because the glass remains easily able to be broken—for instance, by removing the packing material and striking it. Since masks are in this way reversible, they will typically not undermine the ascription of dispositions to the objects in question.

The pragmatic approach to dispositions redirects our attention from metaphysical ones to the issues that confront an agent in an environment. As with affordances, an object's dispositions will depend on what an agent is able to do with respect to that object. These sorts of questions are often simply not specified in discussions about dispositions and their proper analysis. Accordingly, the pragmatic approach says that claims about dispositions in certain cases—especially, cases of finking—are simply not determinate either way. In cases where these details are implicitly specified—especially, cases of masking—the pragmatic approach does make clear judgments, and these are precisely the opposite of those made by the conditional analysis of dispositions.

4.7 On Dispositional Analyses

The foregoing treatment of dispositions is less an analysis of dispositions than it is an approach to dispositions that questions several of the presuppositions in the contemporary metaphysics of dispositions. It is an approach on which dispositions are a linguistically mediated category, on which an account of dispositions falls out from an account of dispositional predicates. And it is an account where dispositions are simply seen as a special case of a broader class of affordances. Finally, and relatedly, it is an account on which agents and the question of what they are or are not able to do is central to an account of what dispositions an object has.

If we adopt this kind of account of dispositions, we can then ask how it bears on the work that dispositions do in many areas of contemporary philosophy. As suggested above, the idea of giving a dispositional analysis of phenomena that are not superficially dispositional is one that has had wide and enduring influence. But, once we see dispositions in the way suggested here, as a fundamentally pragmatic category, what does it even mean to give a dispositional analysis?

Consider for instance the dispositional analysis of color. On this account, what it is for an object to be red is for it to be disposed to look red in normal circumstances. Let us waive for the moment a concern about apparent circularity, as red appears to figure in the analysis as well as the analysand.[21] I want to focus instead on the very form of the analysis, and in particular on the following question: what does it mean precisely to understand color as a disposition, when dispositions are understood in a pragmatic way?

At first pass, we might say: an object is red just in case it is easily able to look red in normal circumstances. This comes somewhat closer to the

---

[21] See Levin (2000) for a discussion of this and other criticisms that have been brought against the dispositional analysis of color.

form of disposition claims suggested in DP, but it is still incomplete. For it takes looking to be an activity of the object that is read, rather than of an agent looking at the object. This is partly an artifact of lexical restrictions: on the view suggested by DP, dispositionality demands a passive construction, but 'look' is intransitive and does not take the passive voice. We get closer to the letter as well as the spirit of the present approach as follows: an object is red just in case it is easily able to be seen as red in normal circumstances. That seems approximately correct: a ripe tomato is easily able to be seen as red in normal circumstances, while an unripe tomato is able to be seen as red only with special measures, such as wearing tinted glasses. An unripe tomato is easily able to be seen as green.

There is an alternative and perhaps deeper way of understanding a dispositional analysis within the perspective on dispositions adopted here. On the present view, dispositions are simply a special case of affordances, and the features that mark them off from familiar cases of affordances are comparatively superficial ones, namely being associated with pseudo-agentive verbs. On this view, to give a dispositional analysis of some phenomenon is to claim that phenomenon is, fundamentally, a kind of affordance. So an alternative way of understanding the dispositional analysis of color is as understanding color as a kind of affordance.

What might this mean? At first pass, we might say: an object is red just in case it affords seeing it as red. This is a somewhat stilted expression, but its meaning is basically clear. As a trail makes walking possible for an agent, so does a tomato make seeing it as red possible for an agent. As before, it is possible with sufficient effort for an animal to see other objects as red. For example, one may see an unripe tomato as red with special glasses, or with special lighting. Yet this is not something an unripe tomato itself affords. In contrast, a ripe tomato affords seeing as red.

There is a strong inclination to say: the tomato affords seeing as red because it is red. But this is not the view suggested by an analysis of colors in terms of affordances. On the most natural development of this view, what it is for an object to be red is for it to afford seeing as red.[22] This is a feature that the present view shares with the standard dispositional view

---

[22] It bears comparing this schematic view to the ecological theory of color proposed in Thompson et al. (1992).

of colors, on which colors are sometimes said to be 'response-dependent.' On the development of this view in terms of affordances, colors are indeed response-dependent, but they are at a still deeper level agent-dependent: they depend on the acts that are available to an agent in an environment.

Another way of framing these issues is in terms of manipulability. There is a philosophical tradition, revived and developed in recent work in the philosophy of science, of understanding causal relations in terms of manipulation.[23] The causal relations in the world mark the ways in which the world can be changed. For instance, since vaccination causes immunity, I may increase immunity rates by increasing vaccination rates. In contrast, even though vaccination is positively correlated with education, I may not increase education rates by increasing vaccination rates. There is thus a deep connection between causation and manipulation.

On the view of dispositions suggested here, there is a similarly deep connection between dispositions and manipulation.[24] A ripe tomato is one that can be reliably used in certain ways, in virtue of its appearance, just as a certain trail can be reliably used in certain ways, in virtue of its navigability. The dispositions of an object are grounded, we might say, in the things that can be easily done to that object.

4.8 The Dispositional Analysis of Mind

When it is applied to the dispositions of options, this broadly pragmatic understanding of dispositions seems to fit relatively well, though it perhaps changes our understanding of what precisely a dispositional analysis tells us. But dispositional analyses have not only been applied to the properties of objects. They have been applied also to the properties of agents. And here the implications of the pragmatic approach to dispositions are more fraught.

---

[23] The core texts for the contemporary revival of this kind of view are Pearl (2000) and Woodward (2003).

[24] This connection should be understood against the background of the extensive connections between dispositions and causation more broadly, surveyed in Handfield (2009).

84   J. T. Maier

We will want to consider, ultimately, the dispositional analysis of ability. But I want to begin with a dispositional analysis that has been more widely endorsed, and indeed may be said to represent the orthodox view of its subject. This is the dispositional analysis of mind, or more particularly of mental states such as belief. The view that belief is a kind of disposition enjoys wide assent, but it interacts in a complicated way with the view that dispositions are fundamentally a kind of affordance.

What does it mean to say that a mental state, such as belief, is a disposition? It is standard to give a dispositional analysis of belief in something like the following form: S believes p just in case S is disposed to assent to p when S considers whether p. We can ask further questions, such as whether the assent in question must be verbally expressed or not, but this rough and ready analysis will suffice for present purposes.

If belief is a disposition of roughly this sort, and dispositions are a kind of affordance, how shall we understand belief as a kind of affordance? We might say something like the following: individuals who believe p are individuals who afford receiving assent to the question of whether p.[25] That is to say, if someone believes p, they make certain acts available to others in their environment, namely the act of receiving assent to p by posing the question of whether p. One can imagine contexts in which this feels roughly correct. A defense attorney who is selecting jurors for her case is aiming to find jurors who believe her client is not guilty— which is to just to say, perhaps, jurors who are disposed to assent to the proposition that her client is not guilty when they consider it.

In general, however, this kind of approach seems to miss what is significant about belief, and about its dispositional analysis. Fundamentally, an agent's beliefs characterize her. The further idea pursued by the dispositional analysis of belief is that they characterize her acts under certain circumstances. But an agent's beliefs do not, in the first place, characterize how other agents might act with respect to her. And we get intuitively incorrect predictions when we assume that they do. A waiter at a

---

[25] This somewhat awkward phrasing reveals the difficulty of even stating the dispositional analysis of mind within the framework of a pragmatic theory of dispositions. Some will be inclined to take this as evidence against the pragmatic theory. As will become clear presently, I am inclined to take it instead as evidence against the dispositional analysis. That analysis can only be formulated in terms of dispositions that are quite different from canonical instances such as fragility and flammability.

4 The Active and Passive Powers   85

restaurant will be someone who affords assent to the question of whether the food at the restaurant is good when asked, but the question of what he believes about the food seems to simply be a different question.[26] More generally, claims about agents' beliefs are claims about who they are as agents, rather than as who they are as objects of the interests of others.

What lesson should we draw from the implausibility of the dispositional analysis of belief, when conjoined with the view that dispositions are a kind of affordance? One lesson would be to hold that this account of dispositions must be wrong. Accounts of dispositions are sometimes held to a standard of analytic neutrality, so that a proper account of dispositions should manage to capture various dispositional analyses without loss. If that is the standard that is appropriate here, then the consideration of belief might show that the pragmatic approach to dispositions is misguided.

But that is not, I think, the appropriate standard for accounts of dispositions. Dispositions are not something clearly demarcated independently of a philosophical account of them. Rather, we are given a handful of paradigms—fragility, flammability, and so forth—and asked to generalize an account from them. It may well be that, once that account is arrived at, that dispositions are not fit to do the philosophical work that they are sometimes asked to do.

That is precisely what has happened with the pragmatic account of dispositions. Facts about dispositionality are shown fundamentally to be facts about manipulability. The appearance of activity in dispositional predicates such as 'fragile' and 'flammable' is shown to be a grammatical illusion, due to the pseudo-agency of their associated verbs. So when we attempt to give dispositional accounts of the mental states of agents, such as belief, on the model of properties such as fragility and flammability, we effectively model those states as being ways in which those agents may be manipulated or induced to assent certain claims. That may be what the attribution of belief is intended to capture in certain artificial cases (for example, the beliefs of jurors in a trial) but it is implausible as an account of belief generally. So, once we arrive at a clear view of what dispositions are, we should hesitate to understand belief in dispositional terms.

---

[26] Note that this kind of objection, if sound, is an objection to the dispositional analysis of belief generally, whether or not we adopt the pragmatic account of dispositions.

4.9 Second Argument Against Dispositionalism

Let us return now to dispositionalism about ability. Earlier I observed that there are two kinds of arguments to make against dispositionalism. The first objects to its extensional adequacy and claims that there are truths about ability that the dispositional analysis fails to capture. The second objects to the very foundations of dispositionalism and argues that the dispositional analysis depends on precisely that which it is supposed to analyze. We are now in a position to make this second kind of argument.

Recall that the following is the dispositional analysis:

(DA)   S has the ability to A just in case S is disposed to A when S chooses to A

Let us waive the various counterexamples adduced above and in the previous literature. I want to ask the following question: what is the literal content of this analysis, if the foregoing account of dispositions is correct?

This is not a straightforward question to answer. Recall that, if dispositions are fundamentally affordances, then the verb that specifies the manifestation of a disposition describes an act of which the bearer of the disposition is a patient, not an agent. That is, the fragility of an object fundamentally concerns its being broken, and the flammability of an object fundamentally concerns its being burned. In the case of belief, we finessed this issue by imagining that belief somehow concerns the act of someone receiving assent from the bearer of the disposition. But it is difficult to see how to generalize this to the many acts that might fall under the scope of an ability ascription. On the dispositionalist approach, conjoined with the present account of dispositions, having the ability to speak French involves affording someone else a certain possible act. What act is that? There is no obvious answer to that question.

So the very intelligibility of a dispositional analysis of ability is questionable once we endorse a pragmatic approach of dispositions. This is unsurprising. Abilities are, fundamentally, abilities to act. Dispositions are, I have argued, dispositions to be acted on. The dispositionalist about

4 The Active and Passive Powers   87

ability attempts to analyze something active in terms of something wholly passive, an account that is bound to fail. I will return, below, to how we should understand these kinds of issues about the metaphysics of activity and passivity.

Even once we waive these concerns about intelligibility, there remains a fundamental point about the order of analysis. This is the second argument against dispositionalism previewed above. Our analysis of dispositions explicitly involves an appeal to what an agent is able to do. To appeal to such a claim in the analysis of ability comes exceedingly close to being circular.[27] Certainly, the dispositionalist aspiration of somehow doing away with claims about what agents are able to do has to be abandoned.

So too do larger dispositionalist ambitions which are connected to this analytic project. One ambition is to make room for abilities in the natural world, and more particularly in a possibly deterministic world, but showing that abilities are nothing but dispositions, which are allegedly an unproblematic aspect of the scientific image. But this project is doubly mistaken. First, we do not in fact have a clear understanding of what dispositions are, and they are more intimately connected to practical concerns than is sometimes supposed. Second, as I have now argued, abilities cannot be reduced to dispositions after all. Concerns about the alleged conflict between abilities and the possibility of determinism, like concerns about the alleged conflict between options and the possibility of determinism, are ones that will have to be confronted directly, as the subsequent argument will eventually do.

4.10   The Grounds of Activity

Earlier I invoked a traditional distinction between the active and passive powers: active powers are powers to act, and passive powers are powers of being acted on. Dispositions, as that category figures in much recent

---

[27] Close to being circular, but not quite. As argued in Chap. 3, claims about what an agent is able to do typically designate her options, and options are distinct from abilities. So one might in principle have an account on which dispositions are analyzed partly in terms of options, and abilities are themselves analyzed in terms of dispositions. That is not the kind of account, however, that we should in the end favor.

88 J. T. Maier

philosophy, do not fit neatly into either category. I proposed an explanation for their somewhat equivocal position within this taxonomy. The grammatical feature of pseudo-activity makes dispositional predicates appear active. Dispositions are ultimately, however, passive. So dispositions are best understood as passive powers disguised as active powers.

In contrast, on the present view, standard examples of affordances are passive powers that are presented as passive powers. The walkability of a trail is a passive power, a power of the trail to be acted on, and that is how it seems to be. So we can think of the class of affordances broadly as a class of passive powers, with a subclass of them—namely, dispositions—displaying a kind of pseudo-activity which disguises the fact that they are fundamentally passive powers.

What then are the active powers? We have already given a clear example of these: abilities. An ability of an agent is a power to act in a certain way. It is not a power to be acted on. That is one reason why dispositionalism about ability fails. Once we reject dispositionalism, we can recognize abilities as just what they are, namely as active powers, or powers to act.

These observations suggest a more general hypothesis about how to distinguish the active and the passive powers. Abilities, we have already said, are powers only of agents. So we might hypothesize the following claim about the bearers of active and passive powers: only agents have active powers, whereas any object might be the bearer of a passive power.[28]

Something like this hypothesis was endorsed by Thomas Reid (1788/2011), who also was quick to recognize the potential counterexamples to it. After all, it does seem that we often attribute active powers to mere objects. A diamond, for instance, has the power to cut glass, and this is the power to do something to glass, and not to have something done to it. Reid conjectured that such ascriptions have deep roots in the

---

[28] Agents might also have passive powers as well. Assuming that some agents are material beings, they may be fragile or flammable just as mere objects are. By the same token, agents may be objects as well. But they are also agents. This is why I refer to objects that are not agents as 'mere' objects—that is, objects that are objects and nothing else.

4 The Active and Passive Powers

89

history of human cognition, wherein, due to misunderstanding nature, we misapplied activity to beings that we now know to be merely passive.[29]

Whatever the merits of this approach as a historical linguistic hypothesis, Reid's approach has significant appeal as a semantic hypothesis. The hypothesis would be that the truth-conditions for the attributions of active powers to non-agents do not demand the attribution of active powers to non-agents. For the core case of the attribution of abilities to non-agents, this would come to—in light of the arguments of Chap. 3—the claim that the attribution of abilities to non-agents does not demand the attribution of options to non-agents.[30]

We can see, at least in a rough and ready way, how the defense of this semantic hypothesis might proceed. Consider again the attribution to a diamond of the power to cut glass. To be still more specific, let us consider the attribution to a diamond of the ability to cut glass. What makes this attribution true? At first pass, we might say, it is the fact that someone—that is, an agent—can use or deploy the diamond in a certain way to cut glass. Put in the language of affordances, the diamond affords glass-cutting. Put in the language of options, having the diamond available provides a given agent with options that they would not otherwise have. These are the facts that make the attribution true, and not the options of the diamond, for the diamond has no options.

There is some plausibility, then, in this semantic hypothesis. A full defense of this hypothesis awaits a general mechanism for explaining how the attributions of active powers to mere objects depend ultimately on the active powers of agents, in the same way we gave—in our earlier

---

[29] *It can't be denied that back when languages were first being formed men were poorly equipped to carry out successfully this investigation into causes. We see that the experience of thousands of years has been needed for men to get onto the right track in this investigation—if indeed they can be said to be on it even now. By thinking about it we can conjecture, and through experience we can see, that primitive people in their impatient and unskillful judgments make innumerable errors about causes. This shows that if it were the case (as I say it is) that active verbs were originally intended to express what is properly called 'action,' and their nominative nouns were intended to stand for the agent of the action, still, in the primitive and barbarous state of affairs when languages were coming into existence there must have been innumerable misapplications of such verbs and nominative nouns, with many things spoken of as active though they had no real activity.* (Reid, 1788/2011, 1.2)

[30] In Chap. 3 we considered giving these attributions a deflationary reading. Reid's proposal is more radical: it proposes that these attributes are simply false, and proposes a genealogical explanation of how these false claims entered our discourse about objects.

90   J. T. Maier

proposal DP—an account of how the attributions of dispositions to agents are really attributions of passive powers under an active guise. This is an open research program, one inherited from the suggestive linguistic proposals made by Reid.

If this research program could be carried out, it would yield a picture of the powers pleasing in its metaphysical and semantic simplicity. Active powers are always powers of agents. Apparent attributions of active powers to non-agents are always either disguised attributions of passive powers to objects or disguised attributions of active powers to some agent.[31] There would be deep symmetries in the ontology of agency, the metaphysics of power, and the semantics of activity and passivity. The larger arguments of this book do not hang on the truth of this Reidian hypothesis, but it would be a compelling result in its own right.

4.11   The Problem of Power

The arguments of this chapter have been concerned with the metaphysics of power, with the question of what dispositions and other powers are. Even to ask that question presupposes that there are, in fact, such things as powers. But it is not at all clear that this is a presupposition that we should grant. I want to close by considering a far more deflationary view of power, and how the foregoing arguments fit naturally together with such a view.

To begin, recall the broadly deflationary approach to abilities endorsed in Chap. 3. We conceive of the abilities as agents as enduring properties of those agents, that underwrite and explain why they have the options that they do. Someone who has the option of speaking French on some occasion has that option in part because she has the ability to speak French. On the theory developed in Chap. 3, this has things exactly the wrong way around. What it is to have an ability just is to generally have certain options under certain conditions. Abilities cannot explain facts about options because abilities are analyzed in terms of facts about options. This does not mean that an agent's options are

---

[31] Note that while passive powers are often disguised as active ones, active powers are seldom if ever disguised as active ones. So far as I know, this question has not been raised in the previous literature, and remains open.

4 The Active and Passive Powers 91

inexplicable—they will typically admit of explanations in terms of certain categorical facts about the agent's knowledge, the agent's physiology, and so forth—but rather that abilities themselves do not do the explaining. Abilities are, from the point of view of explanation, inert.

A somewhat bolder way of putting the same point is by saying that, strictly speaking, there are no such things as abilities. There are simply regularities in the space of options, and when these are sufficiently robust (robust enough, that is, to underwrite generic claims) we count these as abilities. Alternatively, and more cautiously, we might say that there are abilities but that they are simply a reification of options, one facilitated by the grammar of 'able'-sentences. On this picture, there are abilities, but they exist primarily as objects of thought and talk, and do not figure fundamentally in the metaphysics or semantics of agentive modality. On either development, we might say that the account of ability generally is, as noted above, a deflationary one.

Considering the arguments of this chapter, we can broaden our point of view. Does the deflationary view of abilities defended in Chap. 3 translate to a deflationary view of the powers generally? If so, what form, precisely, does that view take, and how does it compare to other views in the metaphysics of powers?

My answer to the first of these questions is basically affirmative. Begin with dispositions. These were held to be language-dependent in at least two respects. First, the question of what properties are dispositions was held to be dependent on the question of what predicates ascribe dispositions, and not conversely. Second, the apparently distinctive aspect of dispositions—how they seem to attribute active powers to their bearers—was shown to be a consequence of the linguistic phenomenon of pseudo-activity. In both respects, the idea that dispositions are an independent feature of the world, which we might appeal to in giving a semantics for disposition ascriptions, was shown to have things precisely the wrong way around. A disposition is, on the present view, simply the projection of a particular kind of '-ble' predicate.

Affordances, on the view defended above, are a somewhat more natural category than dispositions, as they do not depend on the curious effects of pseudo-agentive verbs, but they nonetheless remain a category highly dependent on our representations and interests. To be an affordance is to be the denotation of an affordance predicate. Affordance predicates are far less constrained than dispositional predicates, but they are nonetheless constrained ultimately by our interests and representational capacities. In this sense, dispositions and affordances are not properties that are there anyway, but ones that depend on our representing and manipulating the world in certain circumscribed ways.

So both dispositions and the larger class of affordances are dependent on us, in the sense of being linguistically characterized and interest-relative. This is to some degree an anthropocentric, or more accurately agent-dependent, account of what I have collectively called the passive powers. The passive powers are in fact agent-dependent twice over. There is the observation just made, that they depend on our language and interests, as agents. But there is also a second, still deeper sense, in which they are agent-dependent. This is that the true ground or locus of powers, for dispositions as well as affordances, lies ultimately in the powers of agents.

The reason for this is straightforward. Consider the fragility of a glass. On a standard philosophical account, this is a power to break that resides in some sense in the glass and its immediate surroundings. On the present account, this is wrong in several respects. First, the power of the glass is fundamentally a power to be broken on, a passive power to be broken. Second, what makes this property a power, as opposed to a categorical property, is that it depends ultimately on a claim about what is able to be done. And 'able'-sentences, as we have already said, are made true ultimately by facts about agents and their options. So in this sense the locus of the fragility is not the glass itself, or its environment, but the options of an agent with respect to that glass in that environment.[32]

So claims about the passive powers are always redirected, on this picture, to claims about the powers of agents. And, as we have already said, claims about the powers of agents reduce ultimately, on the present view, to claims about agents' options. This last point marks a third respect in which the present account is deflationary. In addition to, first, holding powers to be dependent on language and interests, and in addition to,

---

[32] Note that this agent will often be a hypothetical one, as there will often be no actual agent in the vicinity of a fragile glass. The consideration of hypothetical agents appears to be something with which we have some implicit facility. It comes into play, for instance, whenever we evaluate sentences such as: 'One can travel to New York by train.'

4 The Active and Passive Powers   93

second, making the passive powers of agents depend on the active powers of agents, the present account, third, gives a deflationary account of the core active power of agents, namely of ability. Very roughly, we might say that the active and passive powers depend on the ways in which we characterize the world and on our interests in manipulating the world, and the only facts about possibility that are not dependent in this way are facts about agents and their options.

That answers the first of the questions raised above, namely whether the present view is a deflationary view of power, and also begins to illustrate the form which that deflation takes. The last question raised above, however, remains open. How does the present view of power relate to other views in the metaphysics of powers? The foregoing has focused on spelling out a pragmatic approach to power with only glancing attention to the issues—such as finking and masking—that have occupied contemporary discussions of powers. Accordingly, the view arrived at is one that is not advocated in contemporary work, though it has clear historical antecedents—notably, as emphasized above (Reid, 1788/2011). Indeed, the categories that dominate contemporary work on powers tend to overlook entirely the kind of view defended here.

4.12 On Efficacy

The pragmatic view is a broadly deflationary, or even eliminative, view of dispositions.[33] In this respect, this view is not distinctive. Many philosophers have been skeptical about the reality of dispositions. The case for

---

[33] To some degree this is simply a question of the rhetoric that one favors. I would say about this view of dispositions something like what, mutatis mutandis, David Lewis says about his own theory of value: *What to make of the situation is mainly a matter of temperament. You can bang the drum about how philosophy has uncovered a terrible secret: there are no values ... Or you can think it better for public safety to keep quiet and hope people will go on as before. Or you can declare that there are no values, but that nevertheless it is legitimate-and not just expedient-for us to carry on with value-talk, since we can make it all go smoothly if we just give the name of value to claimants that don't quite deserve it ... Or you can think it an empty question whether there are values: say what you please, speak strictly or loosely. When it comes to deserving a name, there's better and worse but who's to say how good is good enough? Or you can think it clear that the imperfect deservers of the name are good enough, but only just, and say that although there are values we are still terribly wrong about them. Or you can calmly say that value (like simultaneity) is not quite as some of us sometimes thought. Myself, I prefer the calm and conservative responses. But so far as the analysis of value goes, they're all much of a muchness.* (Smith et al., 1989, p. 137)

deflation (or elimination) developed here, however, is quite different from the standard argument for that view. Indeed, it is almost its precise inverse. Contrasting these two arguments will help to elaborate the view of power that I am putting forth here, as well as to articulate the more general metaphysical perspective on offer and how it is different from more familiar approaches to these issues.

The standard argument for an eliminative view of dispositions is an argument from 'causal exclusion.' The argument is roughly the following. Consider some particular instance of a dispositional property, such as the fragility of this glass. Let us say that this glass is struck and breaks. It is plausible to say that this glass broke, in part, because of its fragility. At least, that is plausible if dispositions ever figure in causal explanations at all. Yet, on reflection, it is not clear that this is such a good explanation at all. After all, the breaking of the glass is fully explicable in terms of the crystalline structure of the glass, which is a categorical property of the glass, as well as the facts about its being struck. The disposition is not needed at all—the explanation in terms of crystalline structure excludes it. The same story might be told for any instance of a dispositional property whatsoever. This is the argument that dispositional properties are systematically excluded from causal explanations.[34]

The second step in this argument is to claim that dispositions have a claim to exist only if they figure in causal explanations. It may be that there are some things that exist even though they are causally inert or do not enter causal relations at all, but dispositions are not plausibly among them. Dispositions are meant to be physical or proto-physical explanations that figure in an explanation of why they act as they do. If the causal role of dispositions is wholly usurped in the way the argument just stated suggests them to be, then we should conclude that there are no dispositions, or at least none like what we ordinarily take them to be.

On the approach to dispositions developed in the foregoing, this argument simply misconceives the role of dispositions in our picture of the world. Consider, by way of comparison, how this argument would be supposed to go in the case of affordances. Walkability purports to be a property of the things we encounter in the world, such as trails. But

---

[34] Prior et al. (1982) is a standard articulation of this argument.

walkability appears to be dispensable from the point of view of causal explanation. If we are explaining why a certain agent walked easily on a certain trail, it may well suffice to cite features of that agent as well as categorical properties of the trail. In this sense, walkability is dispensable from the point of view of causal explanation. We might then conclude that there are, properly speaking, no such things as affordances.

No philosopher has, to my knowledge, advanced this kind of eliminative argument about affordances. And the reason why is that the shortcomings of this argument seem clear. Affordances do not even purport to be properties that figure in the causal explanation of events. Their role is different. They mark off, for agents who are aware of them, available possibilities for action. Their failure to figure in causal explanations of the sort that figure in exclusion arguments like those surveyed above does not even purport to undermine their claim to be properties of the objects that we encounter.[35]

Returning to the case of fragility, the response to the elimination argument sketched above is essentially the same. It may well be true that the fragility of a glass does not figure in a causal explanation of the breaking of that glass when it is struck. But this is not the function of fragility in the first place. The grammatical phenomenon of pseudo-agency may mislead us into thinking of fragility as being a 'causal power' of the glass that somehow explains the genesis of certain events, but this is an illusion. Fragility is a passive power. An object is fragile just in case it is easily able to be broken, and the objects that have this property are useful, for certain purposes, to mark off as a unified class. This is so even if the underlying features of those objects are, at some different level of description, rather miscellaneous. In short, standard causal explanations for the elimination of dispositions rest on a false presupposition about the very role of dispositions.

While I reject this argument for elimination, I do endorse—as noted in the previous section—an eliminative or deflationary view of dispositions and the passive powers more generally. As argued above, there are

---

[35] Enoch (2013) suggests that we distinguish explanatory indispensability from deliberative indispensability. Earlier I argue that options might be regarded as deliberatively indispensable. The arguments of this section suggest that this proposal might be extended, and that the various properties that depend on options—such as the passive powers—might be regarded as deliberatively indispensable as well.

several reasons for this, but the most general and fundamental concerns the view adopted here of the nature of active power. The passive powers depend, as I have argued, on the active powers, and ultimately on the core active power of ability. But ultimately, as I have argued, we have grounds to be skeptical of abilities themselves. Properly speaking, claims about what agents are able to do are true, but they are made true ultimately by claims about agents' options. We could, in this sense, dispense with talk of abilities altogether.

We have now traced a route through the hierarchy of powers that returns us to the place where we began. On one view, dispositions or powers more generally are fundamental, and we give an analysis of abilities in terms of dispositions. I have explained why this view is mistaken. We should recognize dispositions to be, like affordances, passive powers, and recognize the dependence of the passive powers on the active powers, and particularly on abilities. Yet abilities themselves are no foundation for a theory of powers. For abilities themselves may be eliminated, and an account of the metaphysics and semantics of agentive possibility may be told wholly in terms of options. So this excursion through the powers brings us back, again, to options.

Ultimately, then, our view of power rests on our view of agentive possibility. And the view of agentive possibility defended here is a distinctive one. Indeed, it is not obvious where it fits in standard taxonomies and debates about the nature of power and possibility. The next chapter considers why the present view is so difficult to accommodate within these taxonomies, and how to make room for it.

Bibliography

Brancazio, N. (2020). Being Perceived and Being "Seen": Interpersonal Affordances, Agency, and Selfhood. *Frontiers in Psychology, 11*, 1750.

Clarke, R. (2009). Dispositions, Abilities to Act, and Free Will: The New Dispositionalism. *Mind, 118*(470), 323–351.

Dickinson, A. (2011). Goal-Directed Behavior and Future Planning in Animals. In R. Menzel & J. Fischer (Eds.), *Animal Thinking*. The MIT Press.

Enoch, D. (2013). *Taking Morality Seriously: A Defense of Robust Realism*. Oxford University Press.

4 The Active and Passive Powers 97

Fara, M. (2005). Dispositions and Habituals. *Noûs, 39*(1), 43–82.

Fara, M. (2008). Masked Abilities and Compatibilism. *Mind, 117*(468), 843–865.

Gibson, J. J. (1979). *The Ecological Approach to Visual Perception*. Houghton Mifflin.

Goodman, N. (1955). *Fact, Fiction, and Forecast*. Harvard University Press.

Handfield, T. (2009). *Dispositions and Causes*. Clarendon Press.

Holton, R. (2004). Rational Resolve. *Philosophical Review, 113*(4), 507–535.

Levin, J. (2000). Dispositional Theories of Color and the Claims of Common Sense. *Philosophical Studies, 100*(2), 151–174.

Locke, J. (1690/1996). *An Essay Concerning Human Understanding* (K. P. Winkler, Ed.). Hackett Publishing Company.

Maier, J. (2015). Dispositions and Ergativity. *The Philosophical Quarterly, 65*(260), 381–395.

Martin, C. B. (1994). Dispositions and Conditionals. *The Philosophical Quarterly, 44*(174), 1–8.

Menzies, P., & Price, H. (1993). Causation as a Secondary Quality. *British Journal for the Philosophy of Science, 44*(2), 187–203.

Pearl, J. (2000). *Causality*. Cambridge University Press.

Prior, E. W., Pargetter, R., & Jackson, F. (1982). Three Theses about Dispositions. *American Philosophical Quarterly, 19*(3), 251–257.

Reid, T. (1788/2011). *Essay on the Active Powers of Man*. Cambridge University Press.

Scarantino, A. (2003). Affordances Explained. *Philosophy of Science, 70*(5), 949–961.

Smith, M. (2003). Rational Capacities, Or: How to Distinguish Recklessness, Weakness, and Compulsion. In S. Stroud & C. Tappolet (Eds.), *Weakness of Will and Practical Irrationality*. Clarendon Press.

Smith, M., Lewis, D. K., & Johnston, M. (1989). Dispositional Theories of Value. *Aristotelian Society Supplementary Volume, 63*(1), 89–174.

Thompson, E., Palacios, A., & Varela, F. J. (1992). Ways of Coloring: Comparative Color Vision as a Case Study for Cognitive Science. *Behavioral and Brain Sciences, 15*(1), 1–26.

Vetter, B. (2014). Dispositions without Conditionals. *Mind, 123*(489), 129–156.

Vihvelin, K. (2004). Free Will Demystified: A Dispositional Account. *Philosophical Topics, 32*(1/2), 427–450.

Woodward, J. (2003). *Making Things Happen: A Theory of Causal Explanation*. Oxford University Press.

5

A Picture of Agentive Possibility

5.1 Review

The foregoing discussion has defended several theses about agency, options, possibility, ability, and the language in which we speak of each of these. Let us review some of the main themes.

First, I have argued that an agent is someone who confronts, at any moment, options—acts that are in her power to perform, or not perform. Options are fundamental to agency, and so to any study of agents, notably including both ethics and decision theory. An account of what it is to be an agent, and how any agent ought to act, depends on an account of options.

Second, I have argued that there is no reductive account of what it is for an agent to have an option: no necessary and sufficient conditions that do not mention the relation of having an option itself. We can, however, identify certain general principles that are true of options, which I call the Performance Principle and the Possibility Principle.

Third, we can give an account of the semantics of 'able'-sentences in terms of options. On this semantics, such sentences have two readings, and attention to the difference between these two readings sheds light on

© The Author(s), under exclusive license to Springer Nature Switzerland AG 2022
J. T. Maier, *Options and Agency*, https://doi.org/10.1007/978-3-031-10243-1_5

99

100   J. T. Maier

several perplexities in the previous literature. We then give a deflationary metaphysics of abilities themselves, on which abilities are simply a certain kind of reification of our talk and thought about options.

Fourth and finally, I have argued against views on which agents' abilities are to be understood instead in terms of dispositions. If anything, dispositions and affordances should instead be understood in terms of agents' abilities, which are to be understood, once more, in terms of options.

Taken together, these themes constitute a synoptic picture of the metaphysics and semantics of agentive possibility—the kind of possibility, that is, that characterizes agents. This picture may be unfamiliar, because it does not fit neatly into the taxonomies that have tended to characterize discussions of these questions.

One prominent if somewhat simple taxonomy divides 'Humean' views on the one hand from 'Aristotelian' views on the other. The Humean is a reductionist about agentive possibility, whereas the Aristotelian takes seriously the idea of basic agentive powers.[1] The present view, which resists reduction but is also skeptical of any robust notion of agentive power, does not fit into either of these categories, suggesting that our initial taxonomy is too simple. Let us then consider each of these supposed alternatives in more detail, with an eye towards making our taxonomies more subtle, and aptly characterizing the distinctive view of agentive possibility articulated by the present approach.

---

[1] These labels are my own, though I believe they correspond roughly to the way they are used in some contemporary discussions of power and possibility. It is a further question, of course, whether they correspond to the actual views of Hume and Aristotle. I have briefly discussed Aristotle, and especially the key moments in Metaphysics Theta (Makin, 2006), in the foregoing, but I do not purport to have given any serious account of Aristotle's views of agentive possibility. This seems to me a very important, and to my knowledge quite open, project in the history of philosophy—Beere (2009) is one highly relevant recent discussion of some of the questions in the vicinity.

Hume's views on these issues are perhaps more immediately available. Russell (1995), though oriented largely around questions of moral responsibility, is one important treatment. Below, I will briefly consider Hume's explicit remarks on the subject of agentive possibility in the *Enquiry*.

5.2 The Humean Picture

The term 'Humean' is applied to any number of views in contemporary philosophy, of uncertain relation to the actual views of the historical Hume.[2] My aim here is to sort out some of these views and make clear how they bear on the view of agentive possibility defended here.

This task is complicated by the fact that there is not a Humean view of agentive possibility. Some philosophers in the Humean tradition endorse various reductive accounts of options and other agentive notions. The conditional analysis of options is one such analysis.[3] The dispositional analysis of ability discussed in the previous chapter is arguably another.[4] But there is no single unified project about agency that deserves the name 'Humean.' If anything, Humean tendencies in contemporary philosophy seem to be associated with a certain neglect of agency, and especially with a neglect of the idea that agentive possibility is a fundamental phenomenon.

This is, I believe, no accident. The doctrines that are deemed 'Humean' in contemporary philosophy tend to be associated with treating agentive possibility as a marginal phenomenon, and certainly with rejecting the fundamentality of options as I have argued for in the foregoing. In some cases these associations are based on sound reasoning, and in other cases, I believe, they are based on confusions about what agentive possibility is and how it must be accommodated.

---

[2] As noted earlier, I do not purport to give a proper account of Hume's views on any of these questions, but it is instructive to consider his explicit treatment of agentive possibility, most of all the following well-known remark in the *Enquiry*: By liberty, then, we can only mean a power of acting or not acting, according to the determinations of the will; *that is, if we choose to remain at rest, we may; if we choose to move, we also may* (Hume, 1748/2011). If we understand talk of liberty in terms of agents' options, this is a quite explicit statement of the kind of conditional analysis of options that we considered in Chap. 2.

This does not yet, however, provide anything like an account of how the historical Hume fits into the present taxonomy. For one thing, it presents an exegetical puzzle: why should a philosopher of Hume's magnitude endorse an account that is, on the present view, so misguided? One answer is that this commitment flows from deep places in Hume's thought, in particular his skepticism about powers and his view of the place of agents in nature. Another answer, not incompatible, is suggested in J.L. Austin's discussion of such analyses: *In philosophy there are many mistakes that it is no disgrace to have made: to make a first-water, ground-floor mistake, so far from being easy, takes one* (one) *form of philosophical genius* (Austin, 1956).

[3] As just noted, Hume himself (Hume, 1748/2011) is one such philosopher.

[4] This motivation is especially central to the arguments of Smith (2003), where dispositionalism is allied with a defense of what I will presently call psychological Humeanism.

There are a number of issues here, which are entangled with some significant questions, ultimately including the question of whether compatibilism about freedom and determinism is a sustainable position—a question which will occupy us for much of Chaps. 6 and 7. I will not manage to resolve all these puzzles here. Instead, I want to make a beginning on this project by distinguishing between two kinds of views that may be called 'Humean,' and sketching how each of these bears, or does not bear, on the present view of agentive possibility.

First, in one sense, 'Humean' denotes a certain project in the philosophy of mind, which we might call psychological Humeanism. On this view, all mental states are reducible to belief, desire, or some combination thereof. Of special interest to us here is the fact that distinctively agentive states—such as intention, or the will itself—are reducible to the austere materials of belief-desire psychology. The avatar of psychological Humeanism, in the last century, is Donald Davidson, especially the papers collected in Davidson (1980).

Second, in another sense, 'Humean' denotes a certain project in metaphysics and the philosophy of language. On this view, which we might call semantic Humeanism, all modal truths—truths about what is possible or necessary—are true in virtue of certain non-modal truths, which include (on the most plausible contemporary developments of this view) non-modal truths about worlds that are not actual. The avatar of semantic Humeanism, in the last century, is David Lewis, especially in Lewis (1986).[5]

The view of agentive possibility defended here is clearly in conflict with semantic Humeanism. Agents' options are a kind of possibility fact—indeed, they are one of the most common and prominent varieties of possibility that we encounter. But agents' options cannot be accommodated within a standard reductive view of possibility, and specifically cannot be accommodated within a framework of possible worlds, as was argued in Chap. 2. So the view defended here is in straightforward conflict with a Humean view in metaphysics and the philosophy of language. Options constitute, against the semantic Humean, an irreducible variety of possibility.

---

[5] Lewis's writings, such as Lewis (1988) suggest a sympathy with psychological Humeanism.

5 A Picture of Agentive Possibility   103

What then of psychological Humeanism? Here, it not clear that there is a conflict. One may hold that the basic constituents of the mind are beliefs and desires, or states reducible to beliefs and desires, and hold that options are a basic and irreducible variety of possibility. As was pointed out in Chap. 1, this is the kind of picture suggested by simple versions of decision theory.[6] Alternatively, one might take a more expansive version of the mind, and the picture sketched here is compatible with that view as well. Notably, I have already indicated some sympathy with Michael Bratman's view (Bratman, 1987) that intention constitutes a distinct and irreducible mental state, and that view too coheres naturally with a view on which options are themselves a distinct and irreducible feature of agency. So the present view is compatible both with psychological Humeanism and with its denial.

I emphasize this thought because the project of giving a reductive account of options has sometimes been taken to be bound up with the project of psychological Humeanism. The canonical defense of this sort of view is Davidson (1980, Essay 4). Davidson is concerned not merely to uphold psychological Humeanism generally, but also the more specific and well-known thesis that an action is an event caused by an agent's beliefs and desires—what has come to be known as the causal theory of action (Davidson, 1980, Essay 1). Why should the causal theory of action be thought to require an analysis of options? Davidson writes:

> *If free action is one that is caused in certain ways, then freedom to act must be a causal power of the actor that comes into play when certain conditions are satisfied. The champion of the causal theory cannot evade the challenge to produce an analysis of freedom ....* (Davidson, 1980, Essay 4, p. 60)

Davidson is led by this chain of reasoning to the thought that he must defend some version of the conditional analysis that we rejected in Chap. 2. But it is not clear why Davidson is led to this conclusion in the first

---

[6] The formulation of decision theory that comes closest to the metaphysical picture suggested here is that of Savage (1954), on which options are understood in terms of acts, corresponding very roughly to the way options and acts are understood here. The formalism of Jeffrey (1965), on which options are identified with propositions, has been more influential among philosophers, but on the present view it involves an ontological idealization away from our actual predicament (in addition to the epistemic idealization discussed in Chap. 1).

place. Why should Davidson's theory of action commit us to the thought that the 'freedom to act must be a causal power,' let alone a causal power characterized in this particular way—or that the advocate of the causal theory is obliged to offer some such analysis of what it is to be able to perform acts that one does not perform?

I suspect the answer to this question turns on the larger themes of Davidson's essay: that the causal theory of action is somehow in conflict with views that 'make determinism seem to frustrate freedom' (Davidson, 1980, Essay 4, p. 59). There is supposed to be some basic philosophical affinity between psychological Humeanism, the causal theory of action, a reductive account of options, and, finally, *compatibilism* about freedom and determinism. But I want to resist the ideas that these views must go together. The present view is avowedly non-reductionist about options. But it is consistent with psychological Humeanism and, for all that has been said thus far, with the causal theory of action defended in Davidson (1980, Essay 1). (It is consistent also with more expansive views of the mind and with different views of the etiology of action.) Finally, and crucially, the present view is consistent with compatibilism about freedom and determinism. Indeed, it represents the best strategy for the defense of compatibilism. That will be the argument of Chap. 7.

In short, Humeanism has been a predominant view in contemporary philosophy, and it is reasonable to ask how the present view relates to Humeanism. The answer is that it is inconsistent with semantic Humeanism—that is, with a reductive account of possibility and necessity—but that it is compatible with psychological Humeanism (and associated doctrines such as Davidson's causal theory of action), as well as with its denial.

5.3   The Aristotelian Picture

In recent years, some philosophers have challenged the alleged Humean orthodoxy and have proposed to return to certain home truths originally emphasized, in the philosophical tradition, by Aristotle. There are several alleged shortcomings in the Humean tradition. But the one that I want to focus on here concerns the treatment of powers.

5 A Picture of Agentive Possibility

One implication of semantic Humeanism is that claims about the powers of things—the fragility of a glass, or the ability of a person to speak French—may be cashed out in terms of non-modal claims. For instance, it has been argued that the claim that a glass is fragile may be understood in terms of the fact that this glass would break if it were struck (and that this counterfactual in turn may be given a semantics in terms of non-modal facts). The challenges for this kind of proposal are well-known. Notable are the cases adduced by C.B. Martin (1994) that were discussed above in Chap. 4. These cases are often taken to be merely destructive in their intent, showing that a certain form of analysis of dispositions cannot work. But in fact, they can be the foundation for a constructive program in metaphysics, a view that can be aptly described as Aristotelian.[7]

This Aristotelian view takes talk of powers, or at least some subset of that talk, at face value.[8] There are in fact such things as fragility and flammability. These are inherently modal, and are not to be reduced, in the Humean manner, to categorical claims. On the most natural development of this view, this realism about powers applies just as much to the agentive case as it does to the non-agentive. There are such things as agentive powers, the power of a person to speak French or of a carpenter to build a bookshelf. This is to say that there are abilities, and that abilities are not to be reduced to something allegedly more basic.

Aristotelianism, so understood, is in conflict with the view I have articulated here. I have already argued, in Chap. 3, why there are no such things as abilities. Talk of abilities may be true, but it gives a false impression of reification: talk about abilities is not made true by there being things such as abilities, but rather by certain regularities in agents' options. As I argued in Chap. 4, the present view is certainly sympathetic with the idea that the powers of agents have a special place in the theory of powers.

---

[7] Martin himself was a great advocate of such a metaphysic, subsequently developed in Martin (2010).

[8] Perhaps the most systematic defense of this approach in recent philosophy is Vetter (2015). For an overview of the development of such approaches and their impact on various domains of philosophy, see Greco and Groff (2012).

106   J. T. Maier

But agentive powers are something like a ladder that is to be kicked away in the course of articulating the correct theory of powers. All powers, agentive or not, are to be understood ultimately in terms of options. Therefore, views that make powers foundational to their account of agency, as do contemporary Aristotelians, rest their account on a false foundation.

In many other respects, the present view is sympathetic with ideas than animate contemporary Aristotelianism. Consider the recent work of Helen Steward, notably Steward (2012). For Steward, the notion of something being 'up to' an agent is basic:

> *Agents are entities that things can be up to—and that there are such things is a crucial assumption of our conceptual scheme. It is very natural to think that nothing is ever really 'up to' a car or a robot or a planet—that their movements and the other changes which occur within them are entirely dictated by the way things are locally in various respects just prior to the time of that movement or change, together with appropriate laws of nature—or at any rate, if their movements are not entirely so dictated (because, for example, the laws in question are probabilistic only), the eventual result is, to that extent, a chance matter, not something which is truly up to the individual entity in question ... But that things are up to* persons *is a mainstay of our conceptual scheme.* (Steward, 2012, p. 25)

The present account, though it rejects the idea of fundamental powers, is sympathetic with much of this. On the present view, there is indeed a deep divide between agents on the one hand and mere objects on the other.[9] And that difference can be characterized in Steward's terms: agents are beings that things are up to. But things are up to agents, I would argue, just insofar as agents have options. It is up to an agent whether a

---

[9] This is a theme that I will take up at greater length in the Afterword. Note that the present view—like Steward but unlike many contemporary philosophers—sees no crucial divide between human beings and other apes, such as chimpanzees. Unlike Steward, it does not immediately reject robots as candidate agents. It is unclear what gives rise to agency generally, but there does not seem to be any reason to regard being a biological life form as a necessary condition.

5 A Picture of Agentive Possibility   107

bookshelf gets built only if, at first approximation, that agent has building a bookshelf as an option.[10]

In none of this, however, is there any appeal to agentive powers, understood as persisting features of agents that ground and explain their options and actions. As I argued in Chap. 3, our ordinary thought and talk about agency does not, on examination, even quantify over such things. There is no need to appeal to them in a philosophical account of agency. The distinctions that Steward wishes to capture can be drawn more directly in terms of options: agents are beings that things are up to because agents have options, whereas mere objects (such as planets) are not beings that things are up to because non-agents do not have options.

It may be that part of the divergence between the present view and an Aristotelian view like Steward's hinges on a still larger question. In the case of Davidson, it seemed that a defense of the causal theory of action required a defense of compatibilism about freedom and determinism which in turn required a defense of a reductive account of options. I argued that these dialectical connections were not mandatory. The present view is consistent with the causal theory of action, explicitly rejects any reductive account of options, and is in fact compatibilist about freedom and determinism (as will be argued in Chap. 7). Steward, on the other hand, is explicit in taking her account to be incompatibilist about freedom and determinism. On her view, there is a close connection between acknowledging the distinctive place of agency, the existence of agentive powers, and the incompatibility of those powers with determinism. But, as I have just argued, these connections are separable on the present account. This account recognizes the distinctive place of agency while rejecting the idea of agentive powers and rejecting (as will be argued in Chap. 7) the alleged incompatibility of agentive freedom and determinism.

In short, just as the present view departs from Humeanism, so does it does depart from the Aristotelian alternatives that have been proposed in

---

[10] This is an approximation because it could be up to me if, for example, I employ someone who is able to build a bookshelf, even though I myself am not. Employing such a person does not make building a bookshelf an option for me, but it does make it something that is up to me. Such cases suggest that what is up to me is a wider and perhaps more gerrymandered notion than that of simply having an option.

108   J. T. Maier

the recent literature. While it agrees with Steward and others who emphasize the distinctive nature of agency,[11] it rejects any appeal to fundamental agentive powers and rejects the idea that agency is in conflict with determinism. It finds these metaphysical theses to outrun what is given in simple idea that agents, unlike mere objects, are beings who confront options.

5.4   Between Humeanism and Aristotelianism

One way of understanding contemporary debates about metaphysics generally and the metaphysics of agency in particular is as a dispute between a Humean who favors the reduction of agentive notions to a categorical and non-agentive basis and the Aristotelian who takes at face value our pretheoretical appeal to agentive powers. Those views are sufficiently crude that probably few philosophers agree with the exact letter of either position, but they may fairly be said to represent two dominant themes in philosophical thought about agency, at least in the contemporary anglophone tradition.

The present view fits neatly into neither of these categories. Against the Humean, this view takes as basic and irreducible an agentive notion, specifically the idea of an option. Furthermore, against the semantic Humean in particular, this view is an unabashedly modal one. On the view of agency defended here, then, there is an irreducibly modal element to the world, and it is an element that is constitutively tied to agency. The view is not then Humean, on any reasonable understanding of that term.

What then of the Aristotelian? The Aristotelian view of agency, as we have described it, takes seriously the idea of agentive powers, and makes them central to an account of agency. But the present view is skeptical of an appeal to agentive powers, or abilities, as analytic bedrock. For it sees them as something of a linguistic construction, a reification of options that is convenient for certain purposes but does not in fact designate anything real. In this respect, the present view sides with the Humean in taking a deflationary and reductive view of powers.

So the present view is not Humean, and not Aristotelian either. There is no contradiction in this, for these views do not purport to be

---

[11] Another forceful articulation of such a view, animated by an Aristotelian spirit, is Taylor (1960).

exhaustive. This is a point, however, where it is important to be mindful of the independence of the various theses that are now on the table. The present view agrees with the Humean on some of these, but with the Aristotelian on still others.

This point is especially important because of a question that looms over the entire discussion: the question of freedom and determinism. As developed by Davidson, and indeed as developed by Hume himself, the Humean program in the metaphysics of agency appears allied to the project of defending compatibilism about freedom and determinism. On the other hand, the Aristotelian program, at least as developed by Steward, is allied to an argument for indeterminism about freedom and determinism. The present view, however, is distinct from each of these views. So, what is its position on the question of freedom and determinism?

As I have suggested above, and as I will argue in what follows, the present view underwrites a distinctive version of compatibilism about freedom and determinism, one that resists the various maneuvers that have characterized previous defenses of compatibilism. This kind of compatibilism has generally been overlooked in the literature. But I believe this is partly because of the failure to recognize the very conceptual possibility of the kind of metaphysics of agency that I am defending here.

5.5   A New Picture

The oversight of the kind of view of agentive possibility that I am advancing here is due in part to natural imaginative limitations. The Humean and Aristotelian views are rich and fruitful conceptions of the metaphysical landscape, just as much as they are conjunctions of individual theses. To make room for the alternative conception defended here, I want to sketch a picture of the kind of metaphysics that underwrites the present view. This picture will necessarily be somewhat impressionistic, but it will I hope convey the kind of vision of agency and its place in the natural order that I mean to defend.

Begin with the world. The world is a vast collection of spatiotemporally related things—electrons, planets, and everything in between. We have good reason to believe that these things are governed by laws. These laws might be deterministic, or they might be indeterministic—the 'might' here, crucially, is epistemic. That is the physical world and our understanding, such as it is, of our workings.

There may be other things as well. There are numbers and other abstracta, such as symphonies and fictional characters. There are also colors and pains and other qualitative properties. All of this, too, is in the world, and there is no presupposition here that any of it is—or is not—reducible to the physical.

But in addition to all the things that there are or may be, there is also one more kind of thing: agents. We can be sure that there are agents because we ourselves are agents. There are likely other agents as well—other members of our species, and likely members of other species as well, and perhaps certain artificial beings—but we can be sure at the very least that we exist, and that we are agents.

There are in turn various things that may be true of agents. Agents may or may not, for example, be bound to act according to certain ethical principles. But there is one thing that is clear about agents: that they have options, or acts that they are able to perform. We know this from our own case, and we presuppose it in all our systematic thinking about agency.

The world then looks like this: a vast array of physical and perhaps also non-physical things, within which there is a certain kind of physical being that is an agent. And, as an agent, it has options. So, within the world, whose workings we know imperfectly, we know at least that there are beings like ourselves, agents, and that these beings have options.

This is an elegant and relatively austere view of the world, one which does justice both to what we know (and do not know) about the physics of our world and to what we know (and do not know) from our experience as agents. There are myriad things, and, among them, there are beings like us who have options—and all of these may be governed by laws, whose nature is currently unknown. This is a sketch of a view, but one whose details are to some degree filled in by the more formal proposals made in the foregoing.[12] And it is a view that we should, I believe, accept.

---

[12] The distinction that is fundamental to this picture—the distinction between agents and mere objects—will also be elaborated at greater length in the Afterword.

5.6   An Old Challenge

The orthodox view in much contemporary work on the metaphysics of agency, however, seems to be that this view is not even consistent. Here is why. The view above is committed to at least the following three theses:

i. Agents have options, including options of performing acts they do not perform
ii. There is no reductive account of what it is to have an option
iii. The world might be, for all we know, governed by deterministic law

Many philosophers have been inclined to think that these theses cannot jointly be true, and so that at least one of these theses, and so the picture sketched above, must be rejected.

One way of approaching this trilemma is by admitting the truth of (iii) while also acknowledging its incompatibility with (i) and (ii). If one wants to maintain as much as possible of our ordinary understanding of agency, one will then be engaged in the project of reconciling agency with the possibility of determinism.[13] There are at least two ways such a reconciliation might proceed. One is to deny (ii) and to provide an analysis of options that demonstrates their incompatibility of determinism. This was the strategy of Davidson suggested above, and of many Humeans. Another strategy is to deny (i) and to vindicate our ordinary understanding of agency without making any appeals to options. This is a more sophisticated variety of reconciliation, and it may well have been the strategy of Hume himself.[14]

Another way of approaching this trilemma is simply by rejecting (iii) on the basis of our ordinary understanding of agency, or by some kind of

---

[13] Another view is one which does not attempt to preserve our ordinary understanding agency. Then one admits the possibility of determinism, accepts its conflict with (i) and (ii), accepts the significance of options, and concludes that we do not have options—so our ordinary view of agency rests on a mistake. This is one view that might go by the name 'hard determinism.'

[14] The term 'reconciliation' is of course a nod to Hume's *reconciling project with regard to the question of liberty and necessity* (Hume, 1748/2011). On the vexed question of how Hume's project coheres with more contemporary projects, on which it is indeed a sophisticated strategy in the present sense, see the aforementioned (Russell, 1995).

112   J. T. Maier

philosophical argument. Advocates of such a view are sometimes called 'libertarians,' and the strategy might be called a strategy of liberation. This is the strategy of Steward suggested above. Like the strategy of reconciliation, the strategy of liberation is a redoubtable approach to these issues.

The next chapter, Chap. 6, will argue that both approaches—both reconciliation and liberation—are unsustainable.

Reconciliation fails because options cannot be reduced to anything more basic, nor can we give an account of agency without them. Options are both irreducible and indispensable, and so cannot be reconciled with determinism in the manner imagined by Hume and his successors.

At the same time, liberation fails for the simple reason that (iii) is true. (iii) is simply a sober reckoning of our epistemic situation with respect to the physics of our world. It is not even the right kind of thing to be overturned by philosophical argument. (iii) is the sort of thesis that rightly constrains the philosophical project, which is why the idea of rejecting it, as the advocate of liberation proposes to due, strikes many philosophers as a non-starter.

If reconciliation and liberation both fail, then we must find some way of understanding how our three theses can be true together. That is what I will do in Chap. 7. The simplest view, and the one that coheres best with our experience, is that agents have options, there is no reductive account of what it is to have an option, and that determinism might be true. The last chapter explains how all three claims can be jointly true, and refutes some of the most prominent arguments to the contrary.

Bibliography

Austin, J. L. (1956). Ifs and Cans. *Proceedings of the British Academy, 42,* 109–132.
Beere, J. (2009). *Doing and Being: An Interpretation of Aristotle's Metaphysics Theta.* Oxford University Press.
Bratman, M. (1987). *Intention, Plans, and Practical Reason.* Harvard University Press.
Davidson, D. (1980). *Essays on Actions and Events.* Oxford University Press.
Davidson, D. (1980, Essay 1). Actions, Reasons, and Causes. In (Davidson, 1980).

Davidson, D. (1980, Essay 4). Freedom to Act. In (Davidson, 1980).

Greco, J., & Groff, R. (Eds.). (2012). *Powers and Capacities in Philosophy: The New Aristotelianism*. Routledge.

Hume, D. (1748/2011). *An Enquiry Concerning Human Understanding*. Simon & Brown.

Jeffrey, R. C. (1965). *The Logic of Decision*. University of Chicago Press.

Lewis, D. K. (1986). *On the Plurality of Worlds*. Wiley-Blackwell.

Lewis, D. K. (1988). Desire as Belief. *Mind, 97*(387), 323–332.

Makin, S. (2006). *Aristotle: Metaphysics Theta*. Oxford University Press.

Martin, C. B. (1994). Dispositions and Conditionals. *The Philosophical Quarterly, 44*(174), 1–8.

Martin, C. B. (2010). *The Mind in Nature*. Oxford University Press.

Russell, P. (1995). *Freedom and Moral Sentiment: Hume's Way of Naturalizing Responsibility*. Oxford University Press.

Savage, L. J. (1954). *The Foundations of Statistics*. John Wiley & Sons.

Smith, M. (2003). Rational Capacities, Or: How to Distinguish Recklessness, Weakness, and Compulsion. In S. Stroud & C. Tappolet (Eds.), *Weakness of Will and Practical Irrationality*. Clarendon Press.

Steward, H. (2012). *A Metaphysics for Freedom*. Oxford University Press.

Taylor, R. (1960). I Can. *Philosophical Review, 69*(1), 78–89.

Vetter, B. (2015). *Potentiality: From Dispositions to Modality*. Oxford University Press.

6

Against Reconciliation

6.1 Methodological Introduction

We have not, in the foregoing, had reason to talk much about free will, at least not under that name. I have simply given a descriptive account of the kind of possibility that is distinctive to agency, and of the semantics of those sentences that describe it. This account has made appeal to a single primitive notion, that of an agent having an act as an option. The phrase 'free will' has not been central to this discussion, nor have notions like control or responsibility—not explicitly. Neither have the various contentious terms such as 'compatibilism' or 'incompatibilism' whatever theses precisely these terms are taken to denote. The entire approach has been studiously neutral about these contentious debates.

There is a style of engaging in the theory of agency on which this kind of strategy is not always even a visible option. Sometimes it is presumed that we should give distinct accounts of certain key notions in the theory of agency: one of them 'compatibilist-friendly,' and one of them 'incompatibilist-friendly'.[1] From this point of view, one might suppose

---

[1] See for instance the discussion of 'compatibilist-friendly agentive structures' in McKenna (2004).

© The Author(s), under exclusive license to Springer Nature Switzerland AG 2022 **115**
J. T. Maier, *Options and Agency*, https://doi.org/10.1007/978-3-031-10243-1_6

that the present view must be somehow friendly to the incompatibilist, since it helps itself to an unanalyzed and primitive notion of agentive possibility. But this is simply not so. If anything, as I will argue in Chap. 7, something like the opposite may be true.

This entire approach to the theory of agency is, on the present approach, wrong-headed. A prelude to even beginning to think clearly about the many problems that have been called 'the problem of free will,' and the many theses that have been called 'compatibilism' or 'incompatibilism,' is to give a clear and descriptively adequate account of the phenomenon under consideration. That is what the previous four chapters have done for agentive possibility and cognate notions such as ability. Now we are in a position to address those versions of 'the problem of free will' that bear on our topic, and see whether there is indeed a problem here at all.

That is the first methodological note: that any problems about free will are to be addressed after we have a theory in place, and not before. Now that we do have a theory in place, we can address those supposed problems. And this brings us to the second methodological note: that it needs to be shown that there is in fact a problem here, or we must do work to discover what exactly that problem is supposed to be.

In saying this, I do not mean to say that the 'burden of proof' lies with my opponent, the advocate of the view that there is a problem about free will. The idea of a burden of proof, and indeed the very idea of an opponent, are legal metaphors that have no real place in the present discussion. We are attempting to articulate an adequate account of agency and possibility, and I believe in the previous discussion I have done exactly that. If this account faces unnoticed problems, or incurs unexpected commitments, it simply needs to be said what those problems are, for they have not made themselves known thus far.

In the following I will be critical of Hume's 'reconciling project,' or at least of various projects that have proceeded under that name. But what seems absolutely correct to me in Hume's approach is that we should not be too easily taken in by the philosophical problems that are supposed, by tradition, to exist. For often those problems fail to exist, or at least turn out to be considerably different than they are conventionally supposed to be.

6.2 The Possibility of Determinism

One family of concerns about free will turns on a supposed conflict between our understanding of agency on the one hand and certain empirical claims about our world on the other. Like many contemporary philosophers, I think the clearest version of this conflict concerns the possibility of determinism.[2]

What is determinism? Determinism, as I will understand it here, is the thesis that the history of a world and its laws uniquely determine its future. There is exactly one way a deterministic world can be at any given future moment, given its past and laws. Determinism is sometimes presented as a philosophical thesis, to be decided by a priori argumentation, but as I understand it here it is a well-defined empirical thesis, and more specifically a thesis in fundamental physics.

Is determinism true? There are certain results in twentieth-century physics that indicate that our world is not deterministic, namely those results that give rise to quantum mechanics and its subsequent development into quantum field theory. These results, however, need to be qualified in two ways. First, there are deterministic—so-called 'Bohmian'—interpretations of quantum mechanics (Goldstein, 2021). Second, the fundamental nature of determinism, coupled with the unsettled status of fundamental physics, makes a simple and confident answer to this question very difficult to give (see Earman (2004) for some considerations). In light of this, our answer to the question of whether determinism is actually true, at our world, should be that we do not know.

What then is the challenge from this unknown hypothesis of determinism? There are important formal presentations of the problem which I will consider in what follows, but at this point it will be helpful to present the challenge simply and somewhat informally. Consider an actual agent. As we just discussed, this agent might live in a deterministic world, as the actual world might be deterministic. And, according to the framework of the foregoing chapters, this agent has more than one option for action. The challenge I want to consider derives a conflict between these two facts.

---

[2] This is the approach adopted, for example, in van Inwagen (1983) and the subsequent literature that it has inspired.

Assume the agent is on a walk at midday, and that her options include these two acts: turning left at the intersection at noon, and turning right at the intersection at noon. The agent therefore has at least two options, one of which precludes the other. At the same time, our world might be deterministic, so it might be that, given the past and the laws, there is at most one of these acts that the agent will perform. But (it may be argued) if there is exactly one act that the agent will perform, given the past and the laws, then that is the only act that she has as an option. And now we have two claims about an arbitrary agent's options. First, that the agent has (at least) two options. Second, that agent might have exactly one option. And these two claims conflict with each other.

I have taken care to emphasize the epistemic dimension of this conflict. We are not being presented with a conflict between a claim and its negation. Rather, we are being presented with a somewhat more subtle conflict between a claim that we take ourselves to know, on the one hand, and the epistemic possibility of a claim that conflicts with it on the other. So the challenge here is not simply a challenge from determinism, but a challenge from the possibility of determinism—where the possibility in question is epistemic.

In this respect, the challenge might be assimilated to certain other traditional philosophical challenges. Consider, for instance, the challenge from the external world skeptic. I take it to be the case that I have hands. An external world skeptic points out that I may simply be deceived into thinking that I have hands, when in fact I am a handless victim of a simulated reality. Here again we have a conflict between two claims. First, that I have hands. Second, that I might be a handless subject of a simulated reality.

The external world skeptic is not presenting her hypothesis as a fact, but as an epistemic possibility that I should not be confident that I can rule out. In this respect, the challenge from determinism may be compared to the challenge posed by the external world skeptic.

This analogy has value, and so too does appreciating its limits. For ultimately the challenge from determinism cannot be answered as the challenge from external world skepticism should be. And, this, I will argue, is the key to understanding why we should reject what is sometimes called the libertarian perspective on these issues.

6.3 The Libertarian Response

There is, we have said, between the claim that a given agent has at least two options and the claim that (given the possibility of determinism) she might have exactly one. One way of resolving this conflict is simply by denying one of these claims. And, since the claim that an arbitrary agent has more than one option appears foundational to our account of agency (as the foregoing has argued), it is tempting to simply deny the alleged epistemic possibility that she has exactly one.

The libertarian, as I will present her position, denies this claim in a very particular way. She accepts that there is a conflict between the fact that agents have multiple options on the one hand, and determinism on the other. She simply, therefore, denies determinism. More precisely, she denies the epistemic possibility of determinism: she says that it is a possibility that we can rule out.

In a way, the libertarian's pattern of reasoning seems like an utterly sensible one. The claim that agents have multiple options at any moment is a foundational belief about our agency, and one that we should accord a reasonable amount of weight. If it seems to conflict with some epistemic possibility that we do not have independent positive reason to accept, then it seems sensible to reject that epistemic possibility. So a conflict of this kind should lead us to reject the claim that a given agent might have exactly one option.

This kind of response is precisely parallel to a standard response to the external world skeptic. There is indeed a conflict between the claim that I have hands and the epistemic possibility raised by the external world skeptic. One may respond to this as follows: I after all have good evidence that I have hands, so I thereby have evidence that rules out the epistemic possibility raised by the external world skeptic.[3] This response can seem, at least in certain moods, compelling in its simplicity.

The libertarian is sometimes accused of embracing recondite metaphysical complexities. But these metaphysical complexities, if that is indeed what they are, are downstream from a basic epistemic insight, which is that our basic knowledge of our agency can be the grounds for

---

[3] See Moore (1939) as well as Pryor (2000).

120   J. T. Maier

rejecting otherwise live epistemic hypotheses. Her epistemic line of thought goes along the same route as the straightforward response to the external world skeptic outlined above. If the libertarian is guilty of an 'obscure and panicky metaphysics' (Strawson, 1962), this is in the service of a straightforward and sober epistemology.

6.4   Against Liberation

If the best argument in favor of the libertarian position is an epistemic one, so too is the best—and, ultimately, decisive—argument against it. This is simply that determinism is not the kind of hypothesis that can be ruled out on the basis of reflection on everyday facts about agency. It is a hypothesis in fundamental physics, which needs to be decided on the basis of experimentation and physical theory. The kinds of considerations that the libertarian appeals to are simply not considerations of the right kind to tell against a hypothesis like determinism.[4]

The libertarian might here avail herself of the analogy with responses to external world skepticism. If it is legitimate to rule out the epistemic possibility of systematic deceivers and other skeptical hypotheses on the basis of everyday reflections, why is not legitimate to rule out determinism on these grounds? What precisely is special about determinism? Does being investigated by physicists give a hypothesis some special status? Why?

These are important epistemological questions, and it is not clear how they should be answered. The lack of an answer to them does not however undermine the basic point that is being advanced here: that broad scientific hypotheses that are acknowledged to be epistemically possible cannot be foreclosed simply by the sort of considerations that the

---

[4] This objection is articulated with great force against his own position by van Inwagen (1983, p. 210). van Inwagen sketches a couple of ways of responding—neither of which fully answers the asymmetries raised in the text—before concluding that 'this is not a book about epistemology' (van Inwagen, 1983, p. 212). The implicit contention of my argument here is that this cannot be right. Any thorough defense of libertarianism must in large part be a work of epistemology, for the libertarian's central contention is to close an epistemic possibility that appears to be open.

6 Against Reconciliation 121

libertarian appeals to. Denying a live empirical hypothesis is simply not a viable response to the philosophical question at issue.

The nature of this argument is at least part of the explanation of why the libertarian feels that her response is not even taken seriously, at least in certain philosophical conversations. Such an attitude is due to the thought that the libertarian is simply rejecting a methodological presupposition of the philosophical project, at least as it has been carried out in much of the modern era, namely that philosophical theory should be disciplined and limited by what is known, and what is not known, in the natural sciences. A philosophical theory that simply rejects those limits is simply engaged in a different kind of endeavor, one which outruns the more restrained project that I am endorsing here.

6.5   What is Compatibilism?

I have not yet used the term 'compatibilism.' Like the term 'free will,' this is a label that may denote different theses in different contexts. As I understand it, compatibilism is not best understood as a single thesis at all, but as a perspective or research program, with a determinate motivation but with somewhat diffuse implications.

The motivation of compatibilism, as I will understand it, builds on the argument for rejecting libertarianism sketched in the previous section. The epistemic possibility of determinism is simply not open to the philosopher to deny, any more than the philosopher is in a position to deny a hypothesis about the causes of schizophrenia, or about the composition of certain exoplanets. The compatibilist says this not out of any sympathy with determinism, still less out of a philosophical argument for it. On the contrary, the compatibilist is moved by the thought that determinism should remain firmly outside of the purview of philosophical argument.

These considerations of epistemic humility are coupled, in compatibilism, with a wish to uphold our best understanding of agency, whatever that might turn out to look like. On the understanding, the compatibilist is not advocating any particular theory of agency but rather in insisting that our theory of agency remain unaffected by—that is to say, compatible with—the epistemic possibility of determinism.

In both respects, compatibilism is an essentially conservative position. It attempts to hold fast to two core ideas: our ignorance of the fundamental physics of our world, on the one hand, and our confidence in our best account of agency, on the other. It is reluctant to give either of these up without argument.

It is a curious feature of debates over the free will literature that, despite its wide acceptance, there are few positive arguments for compatibilism.[5] This can make it seem as if compatibilism is simply the undefended orthodoxy in contemporary philosophy. It may be that. But it is also a position that has a right to be regarded as, if not an orthodoxy, then at least as an epistemic default. If we are to abandon the compatibilist position, that is something that itself demands an argument.

Such arguments have, of course, been given. I have already sketched one such argument above. The most common mode of response to these arguments has been to show that our best understanding of agency may in fact allow for the possibility of determinism. This is what I will call the project of reconciliation.

6.6 Two Ways of Reconciliation

Let us same there is some aspect of our conception of agency that appears to conflict with the epistemic possibility of determinism. If one is a compatibilist, one might then attempt to explain away this apparent conflict—that is, to show that the apparent conflict is not genuine. This is the project of reconciliation. There are two ways in which the project of reconciliation might proceed, which should be distinguished.

On the one hand, one might attempt to take the aspect of agency which is supposedly in conflict with the possibility of determinism and to show that it is reducible to something else which is not in fact in conflict with the possibility of determinism. If, by way of comparison, someone were concerned that the manifest properties of water conflicted with a

---

[5] van Inwagen (1983) identifies three arguments for compatibilism, but none of these finds wide adherence among compatibilists, with the possible exception of what van Inwagen calls the 'Conditional Analysis Argument,' which is akin to the tactic that I will refer to as the way of reduction.

6 Against Reconciliation 123

purely chemical description of the natural world, then the reduction of water to H2O might be thought to assuage these worries. Similarly, a reductive account of some aspect of agency might assuage worries about the possibility of determinism. So this is one way of reconciliation, what I will call the way of reduction.

On the other hand, one might attempt to show that the aspect of agency which is supposedly in conflict with the possibility of determinism should be distinguished from some other aspect of agency that really conflicts with the possibility of determinism. We can have the former, then, so long as we jettison the latter. Whereas the way of reduction purports to eliminate the conflict in question, this strategy simply relocates it. This is a distinctively subtle and at times elaborate response to our problem, which I will call the way of sophistication.

These two approaches have dominated traditional defenses of compatibilism. Indeed, these views are so entrenched that sometimes compatibilism simply is taken to be identified with these strategies.[6] What do they have in common, in virtue of which they are both attempts at reconciliation? What they have in common is that each of them attempts to reconcile our understanding of agency to the possibility of determinism by somehow analyzing or qualifying it, so that it is the sort of thing that can fit together with the possibility of determinism. 'Reconcile,' in one of its senses, means to restore to harmony. In another, it means to submit to something unchangeable. Reconciliation in the modern tradition has typically been reconciliation in the second of these senses, wherein our conception of agency needs to reconcile itself to the brute possibility of determinism.

I will eventually argue for a version of compatibilism that declines to participate in this project of reconciliation. It can be hard to come to terms with what this sort of compatibilism would be, if one is entrenched in the terms of recent debates. It will therefore be helpful to begin by seeing why the project of reconciliation, so conceived, appears to face serious obstacles.

---

[6] For instance, in a standard reference work on compatibilism (McKenna & Coates, 2021), 'classical compatibilism' is effectively identified with the way of reduction. Alternative views develop different versions of the way of sophistication. The simple view that I will defend in Chap. 7 is not even considered.

6.7 The Way of Reduction

According to the argument sketched above, there appears to be a conflict between the claim that an agent sometimes has two or more options and the claim, supposedly implied by the possibility of determinism, that an agent might have exactly one option. One way of carrying out the reductionist strategy might then would be to give a reduction of options themselves. How might such a reduction proceed, and how exactly would it vindicate the compatibilist project?

We have already seen, in Chap. 2, how such a reduction might proceed. An agent's having an option is a dyadic relation between an agent and an act. A reduction of options would be an articulation of necessary and sufficient conditions for that relationship to hold that do not themselves mention the relation of having an option. For instance, someone might propose that an agent S as an act A as an option just in case S would A if were to try to A.

How would such a reduction vindicate the compatibilist project? As follows. Assume that there is some act A that an agent S has as an option but that she does not actually perform. The claim that this agent had that act as an option allegedly conflicts with the claim that determinism is true. Accordingly, accepting this claim appears to require one to deny the epistemic possibility of determinism, which is precisely what the compatibilist does not want to do.

Here the reductionist proposes the following, accepting for the moment the particular form of reduction sketched above. What it is for an agent to have an act as an option is simply for a certain counterfactual to be true. If the agent were to have tried to perform that act, she would have. But no one claims that the truth of certain counterfactuals conflicts with the truth of determinism.[7] Therefore, the truth of the claim that agents have certain options does not conflict with the truth of determinism either. Therefore the alleged conflict between options and determinism is revealed, by reduction, to rest on a failure to understand the nature of options.

---

[7] On the contrary, some philosophers, such as Hawthorne (2005), have argued that it is indeterminism that may threaten the truth of certain counterfactuals.

That is the way of reduction. Does it succeed? Two distinct arguments suggest that it does not.

6.8 First Argument Against Reduction

The first argument against the way of reduction has already been given in Chap. 2: there is no successful reduction of what it is to have an option, an account of necessary and sufficient conditions for having an option that does not involve the relation of having an option itself. As we discussed in Chap. 2, this is not merely a matter of the failure of any one analysis. Rather, there are systematic obstacles to the project of giving a reductive account of what it is to have an option.

The project of giving a reduction of options has arguably received far more attention than it has returned in philosophical benefits. This project has exercised a number of philosophical minds, running from at least Hobbes up through Davidson, without actually yielding a usable analysis. It is comparable in its scope and in its relatively modest payoff to the equally troubled project of giving an analysis of knowledge in terms of belief (Shope, 1983). Why then has it commanded such considerable energy?

On the present view, it is partly because it was in service of the way of reduction. On a certain way of thinking, the best and perhaps the only way to show that agents' options are compatible with the possibility of determinism is to give an analysis that shows them to be compatible with determinism. It is this deep motivation that explains the otherwise remarkable persistence of attempts to analyze options. But, if the arguments of Chap. 2 are correct, this project is a failure.

Since there is no reductive account of options that is even extensionally adequate, the way of reduction cannot even begin. Nonetheless, it is worth considering how the way of reduction might succeed, on the supposition that there is such an account. For even if we were to grant this, there is still another ground for doubting whether the way of reduction can deliver what it promises.

6.9 Second Argument Against Reduction

There is no extensionally adequate account of what options are. But let us say that there were. What would follow? In of itself, nothing immediately follows. Peter van Inwagen writes:

> *Many compatibilists seem to think that they need only present a conditional analysis of ability, defend it against, or modify it in the face of, such counter-examples as may arise, and that they have thereby done what is necessary to defend compatibilism.* (van Inwagen, 1983, p. 121)

But he observes, reasonably enough, that this is not sufficient. We must also be given some independent reason for thinking that we have indeed been provided with a genuine analysis.

More specifically, we must be given some such reason in the context of considering arguments that purport to show that agents' options are incompatible with the possibility of determinism. For, as van Inwagen points out, any argument for the claim that agents' options are incompatible with the possibility of determinism is ipso facto an argument against an analysis that entails that agents' options are not incompatible with the possibility of determinism. Since arguments against compatibilism are also arguments against reductive proposals like these, it is no good to appeal to those reductive proposals in defense of compatibilism.

Stepping outside of the specific dialectical context considered by van Inwagen, we can draw a larger point. There is a reason why incompatibilism about options and determinism gets the grip on us that it does. There is something in the idea of an option that feels incompatible with determinism. This may in the end be a mistake, but it is not the kind of mistake that can be uncovered simply by reflection on the idea of an option. If anything, reflection on the idea of an option appears to lead us away from, rather than towards, a compatibilist point of view.

The appeal of incompatibilism is a ground-level datum that we want for any intellectually honest defense of compatibilism to acknowledge and explain. The reductive approach to reconciliation does not do justice to this datum, as it takes options to be plainly, on analysis, compatible with the possibility of determinism. If we want a defense of

6 Against Reconciliation   127

compatibilism that is more alive to the seeming conflict between options and the possibility of determinism, we need to look elsewhere.

6.10   The Way of Sophistication

Whereas the way of reduction aims to explain away the apparent conflict between options and the possibility of determinism—and in so doing appears to lose something distinctive to options in the first place—the way of sophistication frankly admits it. Indeed, the advocate of sophistication argues that arguments against compatibilism are, at least in some sense, correct. She makes 'a formal withdrawal on one side in return for a substantial concession' (Strawson, 1962, p. 1).

Put in terms of options, the withdrawal is this. The advocate of sophistication admits that arguments for the incompatibility of options and determinism are, in fact, sound. She does not however deny the epistemic possibility of determinism. In this sense, she remains a compatibilist. Instead, she withdraws the claim that agents have options.

In terms of the argument thus far, this withdrawal would appear to be a total defeat. But the advocate of sophistication does not go along with much of the argument thus far. She contends that we can retain much of what matters in agency without an appeal to options. Specifically, she maintains that we can retain moral responsibility without options, and so can retain it even if the world is deterministic, as it might be. Moral responsibility, then, is the substantial concession that she expects to receive.

The sophistication strategy finds support in some arguments developed by Harry Frankfurt. As discussed earlier, Frankfurt develops cases in which an an agent is morally responsible for what she does even though she does not have any 'alternative possibilities' (Frankfurt, 1969). In the language of the present discussion, these are cases where an agent is morally responsible for performing act A without having any other acts as options. If we concede these cases, then we arrive at a picture on which agents might have no options at all, and yet be morally responsible.

It is unclear whether this vision is one that should inspire traditional compatibilists. Indeed, it is a difficult question whether we should even count

128   J. T. Maier

the way of sophistication as a defense of compatibilism at all. After all, it concedes what to many seems the key appeal of compatibilism: that our conception of ourselves as having multiple options for action can be retained in the face of the possibility of determinism. It is thus appropriate that John Martin Fischer, a leading contemporary proponent of sophistication, dubs his position 'semi-compatibilism' (Fischer, 2002). The widespread appeal of sophisticated strategies in the modern tradition rests, I think, on an underestimation of just how much is conceded, when options are conceded. The first argument against sophistication develops this concern.

6.11   First Argument Against Sophistication

The way of sophistication proposes a strategy: retain moral responsibility and the epistemic possibility of determinism and surrender the rest. There are two ways in which we might resist such an argument. One is to say that the advocate of sophistication has given away too much. The other is to say that she cannot even retain what she thinks she can.

The first argument against sophistication follows the former strategy. In a way, much of the discussion of this book thus far has been preparation for this first argument. For I have argued that options are absolutely fundamental to our self-conception and to practical thought. If agents might not have any options to perform acts they do not perform—something the advocate of sophistication is willing to concede—then it would seem that all of this just has to go.

To make this point concrete, recall the examples by which we motivated the centrality of options in the first place. Consider two points raised at the outset of our discussion.

First, if agents do not have the option of performing more than one act, then agents are never in choice situations—situations where they have a range of acts among which they must choose. Our ordinary conception of ourselves presupposes that we are often in such choice situations.

As a sort of addendum to this first point, the formalism known as decision theory presupposes that agents are often in choice situations. If agents are in fact never in choice situations, then decision theory does not apply to beings such as ourselves.

6 Against Reconciliation 129

Second, if agents do not have the option of performing more than one act, then ordinary ways of evaluating our lives do not apply. We normally measure how well someone's life has gone partly in terms of the options that were available to her, and what acts she took in light of those options. If agents do not have options, then this mode of evaluation rests on a mistake.

This second point may be amplified by reflection on the emotions. Advocates of sophistication, following Hume himself, have placed great significance on sentiment, and in particular on resentment. They argue that this feeling may be sustained even in the absence of options. Even if they are right about this, however, there are a range of our emotions towards ourselves and others that do appear to depend on options. Paramount among these, perhaps, is regret, which characteristically applies to acts which had alternatives, or to options foregone (Roese & Summerville, 2005).

The first argument against sophistication is then simply this, that the sophisticated strategy concedes far too much. If agents do not have options, then they never face choice situations, and it makes no sense for them to regret their choices. If the possibility of determinism threatens options, it therefore threatens much of our self-conception. If moral responsibility may nonetheless be retained, the sophisticated strategy nonetheless requires a vast revision of our natural attitudes. Such a revision was precisely what the sophisticated strategy was supposed to avoid in the first place, and in this respect the first argument charges that the sophisticated defense of compatibilism does not even deliver on its stated aims.

6.12 Second Argument Against Sophistication

The advocate of sophistication proposes to give up something and to get something in return. On the strategy we are considering, she proposes to give up options while retaining moral responsibility in the face of the possibility of determinism. The first argument against sophistication was that she has given up too much. The second argument is that she cannot even get what she supposes she can get in return.

This second argument will depend on the positive account that the advocate of sophistication gives of moral responsibility. If moral responsibility does not require having certain options, then what does it require? Since certain agents—such as agents under duress, or non-human animals—are not morally responsible, there must be some demand on being morally responsible in the first place. The defender of sophistication owes us an account of this demand.

The most common answer to this question has been that moral responsibility, on the sophisticated perspective, demands that agents have certain capacities. What is it to have a capacity? At first pass, to have a capacity is simply to have a certain kind of ability. For example, the capacity to respond to reasons—a capacity frequently cited in the defense of sophisticated approaches—is something like an ability to act on the reasons that one has.

But here the arguments of Chap. 3 become relevant again. Recall that we argued there that, while ordinary 'able'-sentences are sometimes true, there are, strictly speaking, no such things as abilities. If abilities are conceived of as enduring features of agents that underwrite and explain their particular acts, then there are no such things as abilities. If capacities are understood as a kind of ability, then there are no capacities either.

The advocate of sophistication could give us some alternative account of capacities. Or she could give a positive account of moral responsibility that does not appeal to capacities or capacity-like notions. In this sense the second argument against reconciliation is not inescapable.

But it is weighty, and telling. For the advocate of sophistication has given away a simple and fundamental modal aspect of agency—options—in favor of a rather more sophisticated modal aspect of agency. The irony is that the sophisticated aspect may not exist, while the simple aspect was there all along. The advocate of sophistication has given up a lot, for little in return.

6.13 After Reconciliation

The project of reconciliation, whether it takes the way of reduction or the way of sophistication, comes to an unsatisfactory end. The strain in the strategy of reconciliation is not difficult to see. Why then has reconciliation been such a popular strategy among compatibilists? Mostly because there has been no alternative. Indeed, the failure to see alternatives is so entrenched in certain discussions that the project of compatibilism is at times simply identified with the project of reconciliation.

What is needed is to articulate an alternative to reconciliation. If reconciliation is marked by what it is willing to reduce, give up, or explain away, a clear alternative of it should be uncompromising. It should insist on both the irreducibility and the indivisibility of agentive notions. Agentive notions are irreducible because, against the way of reduction, they do not admit of an analysis. They are indivisible because, against the way of sophistication, they cannot be separated into one part that is compatible with the possibility of determinism and one part that might not be. They must stand and fall together.

The alternative to reconciliation, then, is simplicity. Agentive notions are simple in the sense of not admitting of an analysis, simple in the sense of not being separable, and simple also in the cognitive sense of being clear to comprehension. The simplicity of the agentive has been thought to be the special province of the compatibilist's opponents. But it is the compatibilist who is uniquely situated to insist on simplicity.

The basic agentive notion, I have argued, is that of an option. Chapter 2 argued for the simplicity of options, in the sense of not admitting a reduction. Chapter 3 argued for their centrality and indispensability to the theory of agency generally. In the next and last chapter, Chap. 7, I will show how these aspects of options form the foundation for a robust and uncompromising defense of a simple compatibilism that dispenses with the project of reconciliation.

Bibliography

Earman, J. (2004). Determinism: What We Have Learned and What We Still Don't Know. In J. K. Campbell, M. O'Rourke, & D. Shier (Eds.), *Freedom and Determinism*. The MIT Press.

Fischer, J. M. (2002). Frankfurt-Type Examples and Semi-Compatibilism. In R. H. Kane (Ed.), *The Oxford Handbook of Free Will*. Oxford University Press.

Frankfurt, H. G. (1969). Alternate Possibilities and Moral Responsibility. *The Journal of Philosophy, 66*(23), 829–839.

Goldstein, S. (2021). Bohmian Mechanics. In E. N. Zalta (Ed.), *The Stanford Encyclopedia of Philosophy*. Metaphysics Research Lab, Stanford University.

Hawthorne, J. (2005). Chance and Counterfactuals. *Philosophy and Phenomenological Research, 70*(2), 396–405.

McKenna, M. (2004). Responsibility and Globally Manipulated Agents. *Philosophical Topics, 32*(1/2), 169–192.

McKenna, M., & Coates, D. J. (2021). Compatibilism. In E. N. Zalta (Ed.), *The Stanford Encyclopedia of Philosophy*. Metaphysics Research Lab, Stanford University.

Moore, G. E. (1939). Proof of an External World. *Proceedings of the British Academy, 25*(5), 273–300.

Pryor, J. (2000). The Skeptic and the Dogmatist. *Noûs, 34*(4), 517–549.

Roese, N. J., & Summerville, A. (2005). What We Regret Most … and Why. *Personality & Social Psychology Bulletin, 31*(9), 1273–1285.

Shope, R. K. (1983). *The Analysis of Knowing: A Decade of Research*. Princeton University Press.

Strawson, P. F. (1962). Freedom and Resentment. *Proceedings of the British Academy, 48*, 1–25.

van Inwagen, P. (1983). *An Essay on Free Will*. Oxford University Press.

7

Simple Compatibilism

7.1 Compatibilism Without Reconciliation

In the previous chapter I urged us to distinguish compatibilism itself from the kinds of strategies that are typically invoked to defend compatibilism. Compatibilism itself is the view that the fact that agents have a plurality of options is compatible with the possibility that determinism is true. The strategies invoked to defend compatibilism, in contrast, are a wide range of proposals that either give a reduction of options or propose a sophisticated strategy of evading options altogether. Whether or not these are the only ways to defend compatibilism—and I will argue that they are not—they should at the very least be distinguished from the thesis of compatibilism itself.

As it should be distinguished from strategies of reconciliation, so should compatibilism be distinguished from various other doctrines that broadly characterize the world and our place in it. Compatibilism should be distinguished from physicalism, understood as the doctrine that all facts supervene on physical facts. So too should it be distinguished from naturalism, broadly understood as a metaphysical and epistemic thesis according to which the natural sciences occupy a privileged place in our

© The Author(s), under exclusive license to Springer Nature Switzerland AG 2022 133
J. T. Maier, *Options and Agency*, https://doi.org/10.1007/978-3-031-10243-1_7

understanding of the world. Like the strategy of reconciliation, these doctrines are distinct from the thesis of compatibilism and any proposed connection between them is something that requires argument.

I think in fact a stronger claim can be defended. Since the strategies traditionally used to defend compatibilism, notably the strategy of reduction, are associated with doctrines such as physicalism and naturalism, compatibilism itself tends to be associated, in the philosophical imagination, with those kinds of doctrines. Once this connection is severed, however, compatibilism can be seen afresh. Compatibilism is in its very motivations a view that resists arguments that move from particular aspects of agency to claims about fundamental physics. If anything, it is a view that is skeptical of doctrines that too closely merge the manifest and the scientific image. So, rather than being a physicalist or naturalist view, compatibilism can be seen as a view that is at least open to the denial of physicalism and to the denial of naturalism.

This is a promissory note. Articulation of a compatibilism that is freed from the reductive ambitions of much recent philosophy depends on a defense of compatibilism that does not itself depend on reduction, or on sophistication—on the various strategies that I have described as strategies of reconciliation. What would a non-conciliatory compatibilism look like? Only once we have answered this question will we answer the question of what the philosophical commitments of compatibilism really are.

This chapter delivers an answer to that question. I give an argument for compatibilism that does not in any way depend on the project of reconciliation. This argument rather takes as its foundation the robustly non-reductive views of options that have been articulated in the foregoing. The compatibilism thus arrived at is simple, both in the sense of dispensing with dialectical complications and in the sense of insisting on the fundamental irreducibility of agentive possibility.

7.2   Two Principles Reconsidered

The incompatibilist claims that agents do not have options in a deterministic world. To begin to assess this claim and how one might argue for it, it is helpful to begin with a quite general question: what options do agents have?

I have thus far not defended a general answer to this question. I have presupposed that agents typically face a plurality of options in any given situation, and that their options correspond more or less to the options that we typically take them to have. I have presupposed, for instance, that someone with some available money in a shop that sells newspapers has the option of buying a newspaper, whether or not she in fact buys one.

I think this is how things are generally with options. There are no general rules that decide whether someone has an option in any given case. Options are highly particular, in the sense that the question of whether someone has an option depends on a vast range of factors, which may not always be summarized in any condensed way.

I therefore favor a kind of particularism about options. I have, however, endorsed two more general principles about options. These are the Performance Principle:

If S performs an act of type α, then S OPT α

And the Possibility Principle:

If S OPT α, then there is a possible world at which S performs an act of type α

I have argued that these two general principles are true of any option whatsoever. The Performance Principle and the Possibility Principle constitute a sufficient and necessary condition, respectively, for having an option.

I have also suggested that these may be the only general principles that govern options. The simple view of options developed here is one on which there is nothing more to say about options, from a formal point of view, than that the Performance Principle and the Possibility Principle are true of them. At least, if there are further principles that are true of options, then these need to be argued for.

Arguments for incompatibilism, whatever their form, purport to be general arguments about the options that agents have under certain scenarios—namely, in deterministic worlds. As such, these arguments appeal, not to one-off claims about options, but to general principles

136   J. T. Maier

about the options that agents' have. We can then ask: do these arguments appeal only to the Performance and the Possibility Principles, or do they appeal to additional principles? If they appeal to additional principles, what justifies these?

In the next section I argue that the two principles alone do not suffice to establish incompatibilism. I then consider what additional principles might be appealed to in order to complete the incompatibilist's argument.

7.3 The Minimal Argument

One way of establishing the incompatibilist's desired result would be to appeal only to the basic formal principles about options—the Performance Principle and the Possibility Principle—and derive from them the incompatibilist conclusion. Can this be done?

To begin, we will need to formulate the incompatibilist conclusion clearly, in the language of options. Above I suggested that the incompatibilist holds that agents do not have options in a deterministic world. But strictly this may be too demanding. Some incompatibilists, such as Helen Steward (2012), deny that agents even act in a deterministic world. But others seem to allow that agents would at least act in a deterministic world.

But, if agents act in a deterministic world, then the Performance Principle immediately implies that they have options in a deterministic world. Therefore, if incompatibilism is understood as the thesis that agents do not have options in a deterministic world, then the Performance Principle immediately implies the falsehood of incompatibilism, or at least of one common understanding of incompatibilism.

To avoid this complication, we need to introduce a distinction. Let us say that an agent has an *unexercised* option to A just in case S OPT α and S does not actually perform an act of type α. For instance, an agent has the unexercised option to raise her arm at noon just in case she has the option of raising her arm at noon and does not actually raise her arm at noon. It is part of our ordinary conception of agency, as it has been articulated here, that agents have a vast number of unexercised options in this sense.

We can now state the incompatibilist thesis more precisely. It is this: in a deterministic world, no agent has any unexercised options. Accordingly, if our world is deterministic, then no agents actually have any unexercised options. We can now ask the following question: does the truth of indeterminism, so understood, follow from either of our two formal principles?

The Performance Principle does not appear to bear on the question of incompatibilism at all. Since the Performance Principle concerns acts that agents actually perform, whereas incompatibilism is a thesis about unexercised options, the Performance Principle appears simply irrelevant to the question of incompatibilism.

The Possibility Principle is more clearly applicable. The Possibility Principle imposes a necessary condition on having an option. If that condition is not met for unexercised options in a deterministic world, then agents would not have unexercised options in that world. So we can ask: does the Possibility Principle show that agents do not have unexercised options in a deterministic world?

It does not. Recall that the Possibility Principle holds that:

If S OPT α, then there is a possible world at which S performs an act of type α

If an agent has an unexercised option to perform an act, at a deterministic world, then there is a possible world at which he performs that act, provided that the act itself is not inherently impossible. It is true that the laws or the past of that world will be different from those of the actual world. That is what the incompatibilist's arguments seem to show. But they do not show that some such world does not exist, which is all that the Possibility Principle requires.

There is no argument, then, from the Performance Principle and the Possibility Principle to the thesis of incompatibilism. What this shows is that compatibilism is at least tenable, relative to the austere and non-reductive framework defended here. If there is an argument for incompatibilism, it needs to appeal to some auxiliary principles about options, ones which go beyond the bare principles defended in the foregoing.

7.4 Against Restriction

Our simple principles do not, then, suffice to support incompatibilism. Stronger principles might do so, if we were willing to endorse them. Consider the Historical Possibility Principle:

> If S OPT α, then there is a possible world with the same laws and history as the actual world at which S performs an act of type α

If we accept that principle, then the incompatibilist position does indeed follow. If the world is deterministic, then there are no worlds with the same history and laws as the actual world whose future is different. That is just what it means for determinism to be true. Yet, in that case, it follows immediately from the Historical Possibility Principle that agents have no unexercised options in a deterministic world.

Should we accept the Historical Possibility Principle? It is worth considering the argument that might be given for it.

One might argue that, if someone has an act as an option, that act must be possible for her. That claim does indeed seem a platitude, but it provides no support for the Historical Possibility Principle. Talk of what is 'possible for' an agent is equivocal, and in fact neither reading supports the principle in question.

On the one hand, 'possible for' is simply one of the locutions by which we designate options. If someone has the option to go left, and to go right, then going left and going right are possible for her. On this reading, the claim that if someone has an act as an option, that act must be possible for her is true but trivial and provided no support for the Historical Possibility Principle.

On the other hand, 'possible for' may designate possibility simpliciter. That is, an act is possible for an agent, in this sense, just in case that it is possible that she does it. On this reading, the claim that if someone has an act as an option, that act must be possible for her is true as well. But it provides no support at all for the Historical Possibility Principle. It is fully captured already by the weaker principle that we have already endorsed, namely the Possibility Principle itself.

7 Simple Compatibilism   139

The argument might appeal to more sophisticated notions. For instance, one might argue that options require real possibility, not merely epistemic possibility. This too is true, but it too is captured by the Possibility Principle, which requires that an agent's performance of an act be (really) possible if that act is an option for the agent. So this argument too provides no support for the Historical Possibility Principle, as an additional principle beyond the Possibility Principle itself.

There is a further defense of the Historical Possibility Principle, which is simply that it seems true. If someone has an act as an option, then there must be a world that is a continuation of this very world—with its history and laws—at which she performs that act. This is less an argument for the Historical Possibility Principle than an assertion of its truth. Nonetheless, I think this claim does have considerable intuitive appeal, and I will revisit its intuitive force below. The most natural resolution of the foregoing discussion, however, is to reject any restriction of the Possibility Principle. The Possibility Principle itself captures the relationship between options and possibility, and the case for any strengthening of it is considerably weaker than the simple case for the Possibility Principle itself.

We have not found any quick argument from the basic principles about options to the truth of incompatibilism. If anything, these principles are the foundation of a case for compatibilism instead.

7.5   A New Argument for Compatibilism

As noted earlier, compatibilism has typically been defended by the lights of some larger reductionist program. Thus it is supposed that compatibilism is best motivated by, or perhaps is even identified with, the conditional analysis of options. Or compatibilism is thought to flow from a proper appreciation of the 'scientific image' of agency, on which agents are in some sense nothing more than agglomerations of atoms moved this way and that.

Above I suggested that there is an altogether different route to compatibilism. Now we are in a position to say what it is. It is that the Performance Principle and the Possibility Principle constitute the only general principles on the conditions under which agents have options. All other claims about agents' options need to be made on a specific, case-by-case, basis. This is a framework that is constitutionally skeptical of any general claims about agents' options, if these are not one of our two principles or derivable from one of our two principles.

The argument for compatibilism is then simply this. That the two principles alone allow for an agent to have unexercised options in a deterministic world. Consider an agent in a deterministic world. Assume that agent has an unexercised option, for instance to raise her hand. Does this conflict with the Performance Principle? No, since it concerns an unexercised option, not an actual act. Does it conflict with the Possibility Principle? No, provided that the act itself is possible—as it is possible to raise one's hand. Therefore the two principles allow that an agent in a deterministic world has an unexercised option.

Therefore, since general principles about options are valid only if derivable from the two principles, incompatibilism is simply not a valid principle about options. Compatibilism is therefore true. The structure of this argument is somewhat as follows. Let us say that someone claims that a certain chemical compound is impossible. Someone may respond to her as follows. First, that a compound is impossible just in case it is forbidden by the principles of chemistry. Second, that this compound is not forbidden by the principles of chemistry. Therefore the compound is possible.

This argument for compatibilism does not depend on any reductive premises. On the contrary, it proceeds from a liberal conception of what is possible, one that admits only very austere constraints on the relations that agency and the natural world might stand in to one another. These are the constraints provided by the Performance Principle and the Possibility Principle, and nothing more than these.

If one wishes to resist this argument for compatibilism, one might either claim that there are additional principles on options—such as the Historical Possibility Principle—or claim that the alleged impossibility of unexercised options in a deterministic world is a brute fact, not to be derived from more basic principles. I will consider each of these strategies in what follows.

First, however, it is helpful to begin by thinking through the kind of compatibilism that is most immediately motivated by this argument, a compatibilism that proceeds from a minimal conception of the constraints to which agency is subject.

7.6 Simple Compatibilism Stated

Simple compatibilism is the conjunction of two views, one negative and one positive. The negative thesis is that there is no reductive analysis of what it is to have an option: options are what they are, and not another thing. The positive thesis is that agents have unexercised options, even if the world is deterministic.

That is all that simple compatibilism says. It is distinguished as much as what it does not say. The simple compatibilist does not offer any reductive account of agency, or reconciliation of agency to the natural order, or analysis of the language with which we speak about agency. None of these is required for the defense of simple compatibilism, and so are dispensable.

To my knowledge, the doctrine of simple compatibilism has not even been stated in the previous literature, let alone defended. Those authors who have accepted the positive thesis that agents have unexercised options in a deterministic world—compatibilism about options—have felt obliged to defend this thesis by some maneuver of reconciliation. The simple compatibilist declines to do this, endorsing simplicity about options as well as compatibilism about them.

This is not to say that the simple compatibilist has no argument at all in favor of that position. Rather, the best argument for simple compatibilism is one that appeals explicitly to the framework of options described here, and in fact derives compatibilism from simplicity. Since simple compatibilism is so simple, and since it fits so nicely with the framework articulated here, the key question is—why, in light of these considerations, would someone be an incompatibilist?

7.7 Varieties of Incompatibilism

If we are to be incompatibilists, we must reject a possibility that the compatibilist regards as open. We must foreclose a possibility that seems, by compatibilist lights, open. As noted above, there are two ways in which we might do this.

142   J. T. Maier

We might, first, adduce a principle about options that shows that the compatibilist possibility is not an open one. The Historical Possibility Principle is one such principle that might play this role. As this strategy appeals to a broadly formal principle in the logic of options, I will refer to this strategy as Formal Incompatibilism.

We might, second, simply claim that, as a matter of fact, the possibility that the compatibilist alleges to be possible is not a possibility. While it might in some sense be formally possible that agents have unexercised options in a deterministic world, this is not on reflection a real possibility.[1] As this strategy takes the impossibility of the compatibilist scenario as something of an intuitive fact, one that cannot be derived from more basic principles, I will refer to this strategy as Intuitive Incompatibilism.

While this distinction between varieties of incompatibilism is not widely made, it draws a helpful distinction between two quite different defenses of incompatibilism and lets us distinguish the ways in which the simple compatibilist might respond to each.

7.8   The Consequence Argument

The most prominent argument for incompatibilism, appropriately so, is the Consequence Argument presented by Peter van Inwagen.[2] This argument purports to derive, from exceedingly simple principles, the conclusion that an agent in a deterministic world does not have any unexercised options. It is the paradigm of what I have called a defense of Formal Incompatibilism.

van Inwagen initially presents the core idea of the Consequence Argument as follows:

> If determinism is true, then our acts are the consequences of the laws of nature and events in the remote past. But it is not up to us what went on before we

---

[1] This variety of incompatibilism has suggestive structural similarities to the position in the philosophy of mind that Chalmers (1996) dubs "Type-B Materialism."

[2] See van Inwagen (1983). Note that van Inwagen presents three formally distinct versions of his argument. Like others, my presentation will generally follow van Inwagen's first version of the argument.

were born, and neither is it up to us what the laws of nature are. Therefore, the consequences of these things (including our present acts) are not up to us. (van Inwagen, 1983, p. 56)

The Consequence Argument may be thought of as making explicit and formal the thought expressed by these claims.

van Inwagen presents three versions of this argument, and I, like many writers, will focus on the first of these. He considers some agent who could have, but did not, perform a certain act (raising his hand) at some particular time t. In the language of the foregoing, this agent had an unexercised option of raising his hand at t.

van Inwagen then provides an argument for the conditional claim that: if determinism is true, then this agent did not have an unexercised option of raising his hand at t. Since the argument does not turn on any particularity of the case in question, it shows, if sound, that if determinism is true then no agents ever have unexercised options. This conclusion is simply incompatibilism itself.

The argument is valid, and it begins with several uncontentious premises. Its contentious premises, from the present point of view, are these:

> (Inheritance)   If the agent could have raised his hand, and the conjunction of the past and laws entails that he did not raise his hand, then the agent could have rendered the past or the laws false
> (Past-Fixity)   If the agent could have rendered the past and the laws false, then the agent could have rendered the laws false
> (Law-Fixity)   The agent could not have rendered the laws false

From these premises it follows either that the agent could not have raised his hand or that the conjunction of the past and laws does not entail that he did not raise his hand. That implies that either agents lack unexercised options or determinism is false. The compatibilist possibility, on which agents might have unexercised options in deterministic worlds, is excluded.

Any compatibilist must therefore deny at least one of these three premises. Yet each of them appears plausible. That is why this is a good, indeed the best, development of Formal Incompatibilism.

7.9 The Failure of Inheritance

Some compatibilists are inclined to defend compatibilist by denying the substantive premises of the Consequence Argument, either by rejecting Past-Fixity and endorsing the changeability of the past (Saunders, 1968), or by rejecting Law-Fixity and endorsing the changeability of the laws (Beebee & Mele, 2002). Such strategies risk abandoning the core appeal of compatibilism, which is its agnosticism about the fundamental nature of our world. For these defenses of compatibilism take on substantive metaphysical commitments.

A more ideologically austere defense of compatibilism attacks Inheritance itself. This is the strategy suggested by simple compatibilism. Rather than looking to extra metaphysical theses to block the Consequence Argument, we should look simply to the very logic of options themselves.

To begin, we can ask: wow is Inheritance to be formulated, when it is stated in terms of options? As follows:

> (Option-Inheritance)   If the agent had the option to raise his hand, and the conjunction of the past and laws entails that he did not raise his hand, then the agent had the option of rendering the past false or the option of rendering the laws false

The argument I will develop is then structured as follows. First, Option-Inheritance is an invalid claim about options. Second, Option-Inheritance is the best precisification of Inheritance. So, Inheritance is a false principle in the logic of agency and the Consequence Argument fails.

Why is Option-Inheritance an invalid principle about options? Because it does not follow from either of our two principles about options. It clearly does not follow from the Performance Principle, since it is concerned with unexercised options. Nor does it follow from the Possibility Principle. It does follow from the Historical Possibility Principle but, as noted above, we have found no justification for restricting the Possibility Principle in that way.

There is also a second way to think about the failure of Option-Inheritance on the present approach. This recalls the considerations raised

7 Simple Compatibilism   **145**

in Chap. 2 about the limits of control. Generally speaking, our options are in a certain respect inherently coarse-grained. I may have the option of picking a card from the deck and yet not have the option, for any particular card, of picking that card. Our control over the world is in this respect imperfect.

Imagine what things would be like if this were not so. An agent who was not imperfect would have the option of performing specific forms of any act she might perform, for arbitrary degrees of precision. She would have available to her a vast range of acts that are not available to creatures like us. She would have the option of making exceedingly fine-grained interventions in the world. These acts would at least be the right kind of acts to break the laws.

We are not like this. In a deterministic world, our unexercised options are such that, if we perform them, the laws or the past would have to be different. But we do not actually have the unexercised option of changing the laws and the past. This is not because of the strength of the laws or the past. It is because of their precision, and our relative imperfection. At best, our coarse-grained acts imply the falsehood of the laws or the past, but we are not actually in a position to falsify the laws or the past directly.

Option-Inheritance is therefore false. The next step in the argument against Inheritance is that Option-Inheritance is the best precisification of Inheritance. The main argument for this claim has already been given. A framework of options allows us to state clearly theses that might otherwise seem to involve some kind of modal equivocation on the terms 'could have.' Unlike many compatibilists, the foregoing is unsympathetic with the idea that an analysis of modal language can show the incompatibilist argument to be unsound. On the contrary, a framework of options allows us to state the incompatibilist's premises clearly and, when so stated, they are plausible.

Plausible, but not, on consideration, true. First-order reflection on our options and the principles that govern them show that our options do not in fact obey the principle of Option-Inheritance. And since the modal aspects of agency are properly understood in terms of options, this shows that Inheritance itself, when given its best interpretation, is false, and the incompatibilist argument fails.

7.10 Lewis on Compatibilism

The approach defended here bears important similarities to the strategy endorsed by David Lewis in an influential response to van Inwagen (Lewis, 1981). Like the simple compatibilist approach, Lewis's approach does not rely on any analysis of agentive modality (contrast the approach later outlined in Lewis (2020). Like the simple compatibilist approach, it casts doubt on the Inheritance premise. There are, however, crucial differences between the simple compatibilist approach and Lewis's approach that make the former approach the more compelling one.

Lewis proposes that the Consequence Argument trades on an equivocation on 'could have rendered false'. We stand, on Lewis's view, in a curious relationship to the laws as free agents in a deterministic world. It is not in our power to render the laws false. But it is in our power to do things such that, if we do them, some law or other would be false. When 'could have rendered false' is read strictly, Inheritance fails but Law-Fixity is true. When it is read loosely, Inheritance is true but Law-Fixity fails. There is no single reading of this phrase on which the Consequence Argument is sound.

This is a formally compelling response, but it is subject to the following substantive challenge, developed in Beebee (2003). How should we think of the laws themselves? We might think of them as truly fixed and unbreakable aspects of the world. Then Law-Fixity is true, but then it is less than clear why we should not reject Inheritance as well. After all, if the laws are fixed in this way, how could we do something that might imply their falsehood? On this horn of the dilemma, the Consequence Argument turns out to be sound after all.

Alternatively, we might think of the laws as something like regularities, as Hume was inclined to do. Then Inheritance is false, but so too is Law-Fixity. If the laws are regularities in this way, then there is no objection to our rendering them false, on the strict reading of that turns. On this horn of the dilemma, the Consequence Argument is unsound, but the distinction Lewis appeals to is otiose: we simply are able to break the laws.[3]

---

[3] For a development of compatibilism that embraces this Humean thought, see the aforementioned (Beebee & Mele, 2002).

These challenges point to respects in which the Lewisian response to the Consequence Argument is insufficiently general, seeming to turn on issues in the metaphysics of lawhood about which the compatibilist might reasonably wish to remain silent. The simple compatibilist response is preferable, in two respects.

First, the simple compatibilist does not diagnose any equivocation in the Consequence Argument. The argument is perfectly precise, when it is put in terms of options, as arguments that appeal to agentive modals ought to be.

Second, once the argument is so stated, it involves a clearly false premise: Inheritance, which become Option-Inheritance when stated in terms of options. This premise is not false because of any particular feature of the laws or of the past. Rather it is that this is simply not a valid general principle for options. Thus the argument fails before we even consider Law-Fixity.

What should the compatibilist say, however, about Law-Fixity or for that matter about Past-Fixity? Any position on these theses is allowed by the kind of compatibilism advocated here. On the present view, these are simply substantive further questions about our freedom with respect to the laws and with respect to the past. The framework of options allows us to state these issues clearly, but it does not decide them. Simple compatibilism is just the view that options do not admit of an analysis, and that agents have unexercised options in a deterministic world. The denial of Inheritance suffices for the defense of this view in response to the supposed challenge posed by the Consequence Argument.

7.11 The Lure of Incompatibilism

Earlier I distinguished Formal Incompatibilism and Intuitive Incompatibilism. Formal Incompatibilism appeals to an argument to achieve the incompatibilist conclusion. I have argued that the best version of Formal Incompatibilism appeals to the Consequence Argument, which in turn appeals to the invalid principle Inheritance, and therefore that Formal Incompatibilism should be rejected.

148   J. T. Maier

That leaves, however, Intuitive Incompatibilism. Intuitive Incompatibilism does not purport to derive the impossibility of unexercised options in a deterministic world from any more basic facts or principles. Rather, it takes it to be simply obvious—obvious from intuition alone—that it is not in fact possible for agents in a deterministic world to have unexercised options.

The significance and force of Intuitive Incompatibilism should not be discounted. The reader may find it useful to consult her own intuitions. Speaking for myself, when I consider a world where every event is totally determined, it does not seem like agents could have unexercised options. When I consider the epistemic possibility that the actual world is like this, it does not seem that I do have unexercised options. The force of Intuitive Incompatibilism is, accordingly, strong.

We should, however, reject Intuitive Incompatibilism. For this intuition is simply outweighed by the broader theoretical considerations with which it conflicts, namely that agents do in fact have unexercised options and that the world as we know it might be deterministic. These very broad theoretical considerations tell against Incompatibilism, and a local intuition to the contrary simply does not suffice to outweigh them.

Furthermore, the foregoing discussion suggests a way of debunking the intuition that drives Intuitive Incompatibilism. We have seen that the Possibility Principle is valid, but that various restricted versions of it are unjustified. Arguably, our intuitions about possibility can be somewhat coarse-grained, and we do not always draw in intuition the distinctions that we can mark in logic and language. Accordingly, the intuition that drives Intuitive Incompatibilism may simply arise from a conflation of the Possibility Principle with certain more demanding principles that we have no reason to accept. So the intuition that supports Intuitive Incompatibilism is, on consideration, both outweighed and debunked.

Therefore, neither Formal Incompatibilism nor Intuitive Incompatibilism manages to foreclose the possibility that the Simple Compatibilist urges us to keep open: that agents may have unexercised options at a world that is deterministic, as our own world, for all we know, might be.

7.12 Towards a Constructive Compatibilism

The program of compatibilism has traditionally been a defensive one. Confronted with arguments or intuitions purporting to rule out the possibility of unexercised options in a deterministic world, the compatibilist has availed herself of diverse forms of reconciliation in order to blunt or evade the force of these arguments or intuitions. If the compatibilist manages to do this successfully, then a space is carved out where the compatibilist may endorse both ordinary judgments about agency and the deliverances of fundamental physics, whatever these may be. Once that space is successfully secured and walled off, the compatibilist's work is done.

I have argued that this traditional defense of compatibilism rests on certain metaphysical and dialectical confusions. Options are fundamental to an account of agency, and there is no reductive account of what it is to have an option. So both traditional routes of reconciliation—reduction and sophistication—fail. Yet the compatibilist should not surrender. Indeed, the best defense of compatibilism is one that insists on the irreducibility of options. That is the view taken by simple compatibilism, which represents the best defense of compatibilism.

On a traditional view, we might stop here. After all, what more is there to do than to show that compatibilism is correct and that arguments for incompatibilism fail? Sometimes the free will disputes are cast as a debate, where if one successfully defends one's own position and defeats the alternative position, then one's work is done. If this were indeed the right way to think of things, then the exploration of simple compatibilism might reasonably stop here.

But this is not at all the right way to think of things. The adversarial tendencies in the modern free will debates tend to obscure the point of this entire endeavor. Our aim should be to offer a systematic account of agency and its place in the world. In terms of that project, compatibilism is at best a lemma, rather than a conclusion.

When we are thinking this way, then we think of compatibilism primarily in constructive, and not defensive, terms. The goal of the compatibilist should be to work out an account of the place of agency in a world that might, for all we know, be deterministic, and to reconcile that with other things we take ourselves to know, and not know, about agency and about nature. I want to propose that a view that takes options to be analytically basic—the view that I have here called simple compatibilism—is the view best fitted to carrying out that project.

In this sense, while the defense of simple compatibilism figures as the last step of the argument developed here, in a larger sense simple compatibilism is nothing but the foundation for a larger research program of understanding agency and its place in nature, a program which takes options to be fundamental. So simple compatibilism is not really the end of an argument at all. If anything, it is the beginning of one.

Bibliography

Beebee, H. (2003). Local Miracle Compatibilism. *Noûs, 37*(2), 258–277.
Beebee, H., & Mele, A. (2002). Humean Compatibilism. *Mind, 111*(442), 201–224.
Chalmers, D. J. (1996). *The Conscious Mind: In Search of a Fundamental Theory.* Oxford University Press.
Lewis, D. K. (1981). Are We Free to Break the Laws? *Theoria, 47*(3), 113–121.
Lewis, D. K. (2020). Outline of "Nihil Obstat: An Analysis of Ability". *The Monist, 103*(3), 241–244.
Saunders, J. T. (1968). The Temptations of "Powerlessness". *American Philosophical Quarterly, 5*(2), 100–108.
Steward, H. (2012). *A Metaphysics for Freedom.* Oxford University Press.
van Inwagen, P. (1983). *An Essay on Free Will.* Oxford University Press.

Afterword: Of Agents and Objects

The foregoing has argued for the significance of a notion of an option, and its irreducibility to other notions in the vicinity, as well as to frameworks such as possible world semantics. Options are characterized in parts by their bearers: all and only agents have options. So, in arguing for the significance of options, the foregoing has also been arguing for the significance and irreducibility of agents, as opposed to mere objects.[1]

The idea that there is a fundamental difference between agents and objects is not widely emphasized in contemporary philosophy, though it has important historical antecedents, notably as noted above in the work of Thomas Reid (1788/2011). It does however overlap with distinctions that have been more central in the recent philosophy of mind and metaphysics, and it bears considering the extent and grounds of this overlap.

One distinction that has been thought to be of significance is the distinction between living and non-living beings. Peter van Inwagen, for instance, argues that the only composite beings that exist are living beings (van Inwagen, 1990). Another distinction is the distinction between animals and non-animals. As we have already noted, this is a distinction

---

[1] As I have already noted, the qualifier 'mere' is needed since agents too may be objects, having properties such as mass and shape. I omit it in what follows and use 'objects' narrowly to designate objects that are not also agents.

© The Author(s), under exclusive license to Springer Nature Switzerland AG 2022 **151**
J. T. Maier, *Options and Agency*, https://doi.org/10.1007/978-3-031-10243-1

152   Afterword: Of Agents and Objects

underscores in Helen Steward's advocacy of expanding the realm of the philosophy of agency beyond human beings, an expansion with which the present account is deeply sympathetic.

Despite these sympathies, neither the distinction between living and non-living beings nor the distinction between animals and non-animals necessarily coincides with the distinction between agents and non-agents. The class of living beings is almost certainly too broad: plants are living beings, but they do not have options. The class of animals may not be too broad, in the sense that every animal has options, but it is almost certainly too narrow. If we take seriously the possibility of embodied artificial intelligences—robots, in some sense of that term—then we must take seriously the at least theoretical possibility of beings who have options who are not animals.

So the distinction between agents and objects is not to be identified with either the distinction between living and non-living beings or the distinction between animals and non-animals. These distinctions are, as it were, too biological to adequately capture the bounds of agency and of non-agency. If we want to identify the distinction between agents and objects with some other distinction, we need to look elsewhere.

It is natural to seek this distinction in the philosophy of mind. The sort of beings who make trouble for a purely biological account of agency have been given extensive attention within the recent study of mind. We might for example consider the distinction between beings who have representation states, in some sense of that term, and those that do not. Or we might, if this is in fact a different distinction, consider the distinction between beings who have phenomenal consciousness, and those that do not.

I think these distinctions have a better claim to extensional adequacy than do the more biological distinctions canvassed above. But they are still wide of the mark. The argument against them was foreshadowed in our earlier arguments against the conditional analysis of options. There I argued that an agent might have options even if she did not have the cognitive states that the analysis required, that agent might still have options. For instance, against the proposal that an agent has an act A as an option just in case she would A if she intended to, I suggested that an agent might have options even if she did not have the right cognitive architecture for the ascription of intention.

Afterword: Of Agents and Objects   153

That argument moved from the free recombination of psychological states to the simplicity of options, while the present argument moves in the opposite direction. As options are simple and unanalyzable, they can in principle be present or absent from any specific cognitive arrangement. It does seem like there is some correlation between having options and having some degree of cognitive sophistication, but this does not suffice to make any particular distinction drawn in terms of cognition align with the distinction between agents and objects.

Matters are similar when we turn from cognition to phenomenal consciousness. The hypothesis that all and only agents have phenomenal consciousness is pleasing in its simplicity. But it does not appear to be one that we have reason to believe. And the more exotic scenarios in the literature on phenomenal consciousness make trouble for this simple hypothesis. The panpsychist asserts precisely that mere objects are bearers of phenomenal consciousness (Skrbina, 2005). And if one admits the metaphysical possibility of 'zombies'—creatures who have the same cognitive states as us but lack phenomenal consciousness (Chalmers, 1996)—one would thereby seem to sever the connection between agency and phenomenal consciousness, assuming that a zombie would still have options.[2]

It may turn out that some distinction in the philosophy of mind is coextensive with the distinction between agents and objects. But an initial consideration of these distinctions suggests that these distinctions are distinct, in the sense that there are possible scenarios where they fail to overlap. This is underwritten by the simplicity of options. Since options do not admit of an analysis in terms of psychology, a variety of psychologies can allow the presence, or absence, of options. And since a being is an agent just in case it has options, it follows that agency resists any simple characterization in terms of psychology.

I have not considered some other distinctions that are sometimes taken to be relevant. One is the distinction between beings that are morally

---

[2] One might deny this assumption, and the result would be an intriguing philosophy of mind and action. On this picture, options would not supervene on the physical, and a world in which agents lack consciousness would also be one in which they were not able to do anything but what they actually do. The following discussion does not reject this intriguing possibility, though it does not adopt it either.

responsible, or capable of being morally responsible, and those that are not. As I have argued at various points, this is not a distinction that we should take to be coextensive with agency. It may be that only agents are held to be morally responsible.[3] But the category of morally responsible beings is nonetheless far too narrow than that of agents: mice and other rodents, for instance, have options for action, but they are typically held to be morally responsible. This is why, as I have argued, the notion of moral responsibility cannot be expected to play a foundational role in the philosophy of agency: it is, for one thing, simply too narrow.[4]

The distinction between agents and mere objects is therefore not to be identified with various other distinctions in the vicinity. It does not appear to even coincide with any of these distinctions, at least not across the range of what is possible. In addition, the distinction between agents and mere objects has a strong claim to being more significant than the various distinctions canvassed above. It is difficult to adjudicate whether one distinction is more or less significant than another, but I want to make the case that the distinction between agents and non-agents has as good a claim as any to being regarded as a basic one.

To begin, this distinction is marked semantically. The notion of an agent and the correlative category of grammatical voice is observed in every natural language and can reasonably be regarded as one of the fundamental linguistic categories (Klaiman, 1991). The grammatical notion of voice encompasses more than agents, as was noted earlier in Chap. 4. Thus, for instance, 'Everest rises above the valley' may be true, with Everest as the subject of an active verb, even though Everest is not an agent, and 'rises' in this context does not denote an act. As we suggested earlier, however, and as was suggested by Thomas Reid (1788/2011), this does not show that the distinction between agency and non-agency is not

---

[3] One possibly problematic case is 'collective responsibility' (Giubilini & Levy, 2018): one might hold that industrialized nations are collectively responsible for global warming, and yet not think that these nations constitute an agent.

[4] There are other reasons as well. One, identified earlier, is that agency occurs in all of our acts and omissions, while moral responsibility seems to arise for only a few of them. So moral responsibility is too narrow even when we fix our attention to the human species. Another, more contentious, is that there are cultures whose presuppositions about moral responsibility are altogether from our own (Williams, 1992), suggesting that our own standards of moral responsibility do not apply everywhere, while the basic elements of agency, on the present picture, are universal.

Afterword: Of Agents and Objects **155**

linguistically marked. Rather, it shows that the category is marked at best roughly, and the aim of philosophical understanding should be to retain the distinction but to sharpen our sense of its boundaries.

The distinction is also marked cognitively. Children draw the distinction between agents and non-agents relatively early in their development and deploy it with ready facility.[5] As with the linguistic distinction between agency and non-agency, this distinction is often drawn incorrectly, often with great effect: children's toys and stories draw on the charm and mystery of non-agents who seem to be agents. This is a distinction that individuals get better and better at drawing, and the kind of philosophical account of agency developed in the foregoing may be thought of as continuous with our pretheoretical practices of recognizing the bounds of agency.

This distinction is marked, finally, phenomenally. The sense of agency is a well-studied mechanism by which the agent is immediately aware of the difference between her doing something (for instance, her raising her arm) and it simply happening of its own accord (her arm going up, perhaps due to some external stimulus).[6] It is difficult to articulate how to understand the sense of agency, and how to reconcile it with forms of perceptual awareness, such as sight, that have been foregrounded in the philosophical tradition. However precisely this is done, the very existence of a sense of agency indicates that the distinction between agent and mere object shows up in our most basic perceptual encounters with the world and with ourselves.[7]

It might be said that, while the distinction between agency and non-agency is linguistically and psychologically basic, it is not metaphysically basic. There are various ways of developing this claim, depending on one's preferred interpretation of the honorific 'metaphysical.' One thought is that agency does not show up in the natural sciences, especially

---

[5] Poulin-Dubois et al. (1996) show, for instance, that infants reliably discriminate between the surprising self-propulsion of a robot and the unsurprising self-propulsion of a human being as early as nine months.

[6] Wegner (2002) provides a survey of the relevant research, as well as a more tendentious account of its philosophical significance.

[7] One philosopher who is alive to this encounter with the merely objective and its centrality to the theory of perception is Fichte, in his discussion of the *Anstoss* (Breazeale, 2013).

156 Afterword: Of Agents and Objects

not in physics, and that metaphysics ought to be in some sense continuous with physics. Another thought, not necessarily distinct, proceeds from some account of what is to be counted as fundamental, and argues that agency is not fundamental in these terms.[8]

These kinds of concerns about the distinction between agents and mere objects come in more and less radical varieties. On a less radical development, we might acknowledge the distinction between agents and objects but deny it is a fundamental one, on some understanding of fundamentality. On a more radical development, we might reject the distinction altogether, perhaps by arguing that agents do not, strictly speaking, exist, so that everything is a mere object after all. One might for instance claim that we do not need to quantify over agents in our best explanations, that a proper scientific account of the world can therefore leave out agents, and so that there are no such things but mere objects after all.[9]

These are deep concerns, and I think their influence and power helps to explain the relative neglect of agency within the analytic metaphysics of the last century.[10] One way of responding to them would be by securing a place for agents within the scientific image. The philosophical program of defending 'agent causation' may be regarded as an attempt to do precisely that. Another way of responding, however, is simply to reject the conception of metaphysics on which these concerns ultimately rest. This is the way adopted here. There might be things that are fundamental that nonetheless do not show up from the perspective of physics or of the natural sciences generally. That is just what agents are like.

As I have said, this position is idiosyncratic from the point of view of recent analytic metaphysics, but it constitutes a prominent tradition in

---

[8] See Sider (2011) for one recent articulation of this kind of approach.

[9] This would be an argument for an error theory about agency pursued along the lines of Gilbert Harman's famous challenge to morality in Harman (1977). And one way to respond to this argument, while accepting its presuppositions, would be to endorse an idea we have already encountered, and to take agents themselves to in some sense be causes. As I will argue presently, I believe this strategy concedes far too much to the skeptic about agency.

[10] An exception here is the 'problem of free will,' which is a staple of this tradition in metaphysics, with van Inwagen (1983) serving as its locus classicus. On the present view, this is an approach that is bound to be incomplete, as the correct approach to this problem, and indeed an understanding of how to even state the problem, rests on an understanding of agency more broadly, in a way that I have charted in the foregoing discussion.

Afterword: Of Agents and Objects 157

the history of philosophy. Some of the authors who have advocated for an agent-centric metaphysics have already been mentioned in the foregoing: Aristotle (Makin, 2006), Thomas Reid (1788/2011), and Jean-Paul Sartre (1956) are radically different from one another, but each of them takes agency to be a fundamental notion in his metaphysics.[11]

I want then to suggest, as something like a closing hypothesis, the idea that the boundary between agents and mere objects is a basic one for comprehending much that is of philosophical interest. Since an agent is a being with options, this very same point can be stated in terms of options: the boundary between beings that have options and those that do not is a basic one for comprehending much that is of philosophical interest. On either of these formulations, this hypothesis can be thought of as an organizing principle for much of the proceeding discussion.

Begin with the discussion, in the Introduction, of the philosophy of agency. There I advocated taking the philosophy of agency, as opposed to the philosophy of action, as a natural category for philosophical study. Action, I argued, was simply one particular aspect of agency, and not necessarily the most significant one. The hypothesis at hand gives further support for this idea. If the boundary between agents and objects is a basic one, it follows that the philosophy of agency is a natural area for philosophical study. Indeed, we might think of metaphysics as traditionally conceived as subdividing into two areas of study: the philosophy of objects (consisting of questions about composition, persistence, universals, and so forth) and the philosophy of agency.

Consider then the arguments of Chaps. 2 and 3, on which options represent a sui generis variety of possibility and 'able'-sentences are made true by claims about agents' options. Superficially, it can seem curious that there is a kind of possibility that is distinctive. Is there also a kind of possibility that is distinctive to coffee cups, or to paper clips? It is this kind of thought that has led many philosophers to suppose that agentive possibility might be modeled as some kind of 'restriction' on the more general variety of possibility articulated in possible worlds semantics. I argued in Chap. 2 why such strategies do not work. We can now, in light

---

[11] Arguably Schopenhauer (1844/1966) is yet another philosopher who takes agency, in a sufficiently broad sense of that term, to be fundamental to a proper account of the world as we find it.

158   Afterword: Of Agents and Objects

of the hypothesis that the distinction between agents and objects is basic, articulate a deeper reason. It makes sense, or at least is not altogether surprising, that there is a kind of possibility that is distinctive to agents. For agents are not, like coffee cups and paper clips, simply one object among others. They are a basic variety of being, and as such involve a basic variety of possibility.

The hypothesis also lends some context to the focus of Chap. 3, namely 'able'-sentences. Again, it might seem odd that this one fragment of modal language calls for special treatment. But, on the thought that agency is a basic category, this makes more sense. 'Able'-sentences call for special treatment because they are especially tied to agency. Indeed, the existence of such sentences is further support for the suggestion that the distinction between agency and non-agency is semantically marked, not only in the device of voice but also in the lexicon itself.

The thought that there is a fundamental distinction between agents and mere objects bears especially closely on the arguments of Chaps. 4 and 5. The standard way of discussing powers in contemporary metaphysics is roughly as follows: there are a variety of powers, with dispositions representing the core case and other powers, including affordances and abilities, being relatively marginal. Indeed, affordances (Scarantino, 2003) and abilities (Vihvelin, 2004) may well be modeled as special kinds of dispositions. This is not a line of inquiry on which the distinction between agents and objects is an especially salient one. Indeed, the effect of certain proposals in this area (notably dispositionalism about ability) is precisely to elide it.

As I argued, this essentially homogenous approach to the powers suppresses a distinction that has been historically central to philosophical thought about these topics: the distinction between active and passive powers. I argued for revitalizing this distinction, and for taking care to distinguish grammatical activity from metaphysical activity. Dispositional predicates involve the first of these but not the second. Once we have a clear view of these issues, we arrive at an elegant view: only agents have active powers, whereas mere objects have only passive powers. Further, the active powers of agents are in some sense prior to the passive powers of objects, since the ascription of powers to objects always makes

Afterword: Of Agents and Objects 159

reference to the representations and interests of the agents who are able to manipulate those objects.

This view of powers aligns deeply with the hypothesis that the distinction between agents and objects is basic. Contemporary discussions of power, unmindful of this distinction, lose track of the historical distinction between active and passive powers. The present view of power therefore, as I argued in Chap. 5, fits neatly into neither of the categories that predominate in contemporary metaphysics: it is neither 'Humean' nor 'Aristotelian.' But this does not reflect a shortcoming in the account. Rather, it reflects the limitations of contemporary views of the material world, on which agents are often, explicitly or implicitly, lumped together with mere objects.

In several ways, then, the distinction between agents and mere objects has been a thread connecting the arguments of this book. The hypothesis that the distinction should be regarded as a philosophically basic one is something of a background theme for these arguments. In fact, the ideas of this book—that agency precedes action, that options are basic, and that the active powers are prior to the passive powers—can be thought of as supporting this larger hypothesis.

I think the distinction between agents and objects is especially useful in appreciating the problem that occupied us in Chaps. 6 and 7: this was the problem of free will, in at least one sense of that phrase. I emphasized that this problem—that is, the version of the problem that I intended to discuss, and also one that has been historically prominent—was not in the first place a problem about moral responsibility, or about whether the demands for moral responsibility were met in a deterministic world. Instead, it was a problem about options, and their relationship to the world as it is described in physics. Specifically: is the conviction that agents have unexercised options compatible with ignorance about whether the actual world is deterministic? The compatibilist contends that it is, and Chap. 6 built on our earlier discussion of options to develop a simple yet uncompromising defense of compatibilism.

I want to close by reconsidering these questions in light of the distinction between agents and mere objects. The reconsideration does not require revision of any of the arguments of Chaps. 6 and 7, but it puts them in a different, and perhaps more general, setting. In the earlier

160   Afterword: Of Agents and Objects

discussion pointed out that the program of compatibilism is often associated, in the philosophical imagination with the program of giving an analysis of options. This is unfortunate on several counts. First, since options in fact do not admit of an analysis, it foredooms compatibilism to failure. Second, there is in fact no logical connection between compatibilism and this analytic program. Third and finally, the best defense of compatibilism—the view that I called simple compatibilism—is one that explicitly rejects the analysis of options. So one of the most influential tendencies in the defense of compatibilism has in fact proceeded in precisely the wrong direction.

From a broader point of view, however, the question of whether options admit of an analysis may not fully capture the deeper convictions that animate the free will debate. After all, the question of whether options admit of an analysis is a question on which scarcely anyone who is not involved in these questions has an opinion. Yet the debate between the compatibilist and incompatibilist appears to touch on deep convictions, as does the lure of incompatibilism described in Chap. 7. Therefore, if we want to capture the thinking that captures that conflict, as well as chart where the compatibilist has tended to go wrong, we want to move to a more general question.

That question, I want to suggest, is whether there is a basic distinction between agents and objects. The free will debate, after all, appears ultimately to concern the place of agents in the natural order. The first question for understanding this debate, then, is: are agents fundamentally like other elements of nature, or are they fundamentally different from them? This question is seldom asked explicitly, although it is often answered implicitly. Indeed, their different answers to it mark a defining contrast between the compatibilist and the incompatibilist.

Begin with the incompatibilist. Many central defenses of incompatibilism are built around the idea that agency is somehow a metaphysically distinctive phenomenon: agent causation, for example, is perhaps the clearest instance of a view that takes agency to be metaphysically distinctive (though someone who takes agency to be metaphysically distinctive is not obliged to endorse agent causation). More generally, the very idea of incompatibilism seems to turn on a presupposition about the

Afterword: Of Agents and Objects   **161**

distinctiveness of agency. No one supposes that the fragility of glasses or the walkability of trails poses a special question about the truth of determinism. Only if agents are somehow distinctive does incompatibilism even become a salient thought.[12]

Consider then the compatibilist. The idea that agents are not, in fact, distinctive from other elements of the natural order is a central theme of compatibilism in both its historical and its contemporary formulations.[13] This makes sense. If the case for incompatibilism arises only under the presupposition that agents are somehow metaphysically distinctive, then the most direct route to a defense of compatibilism would appear to be a denial of that presupposition.

The way out of this dialectic, I believe, is precisely to concede to the incompatibilist the basic distinction between agents and objects, but to deny that the incompatibilist conclusion follows. For all the reasons we have already given, the incompatibilist is right to insist on the basic difference between agents and objects. Among all the beings that there are

---

[12] It is notable that this asymmetry is often unquestioned in contemporary discussions of powers. The entire project of dispositionalism about ability, for instance, rests on the curious and largely undefended assumption that dispositions are clearly compatible with determinism whereas abilities are sometimes thought not to be. Since both dispositions and abilities seem to imply happenings outside of the actual sequence of events, why should not they be thought equally problematic with respect to the possibility of determinism? One thought is that it is really moral responsibility that is supposed to be in tension with determinism, and it is their connection to moral responsibility that explains the special problems posed by abilities and by agentive possibility more generally I have already explained why I hold moral responsibility to be a poor candidate for marking a foundational distinction. Even waiving that point, however, this does not really answer the question. As we have seen, standard arguments proceed by arguing that moral responsibility is supposed to depend on agentive possibility, and agentive possibility is supposed to be in conflict with determinism—but why is agentive possibility supposed to be problematic in a way that dispositional possibility is not?

I hold, as does Steward (2012), that the philosophical tradition here is implicitly recognizing something that it often fails to acknowledge explicitly: that agency poses a special metaphysical problem, in a way that mere objects do not. As it happens, I argue (unlike Steward), that ultimately this very distinction collapses. As the dispositions and affordances of objects depend, ultimately, on the powers of agents with respect to those objects, if determinism were to threaten agentive possibility, it might threaten ontic possibility quite generally. But, as it happens, it does not, for simple compatibilism is true.

[13] See Dennett (1984), for instance, for an extended articulation of this perspective on the traditional problem of free will.

in the world, there is one kind of being, and agent, that is special. Unlike other beings, an agent acts, and it faces a plurality of options for action, only some of which it takes. Among a world of things that are simply moved about by forces beyond their control, the agent is a locus of real possibility.

These sentiments are so strongly associated with the incompatibilist conception of the world that they can seem to be tantamount to an assertion of incompatibilism. Yet they are not. Each of these claims is literally true. Yet compatibilism is true as well. How is that possible? Compatibilism, recall, is the proposition that agents have unexercised options and determinism might be true. And that proposition is altogether consistent with claim that agency is a metaphysically distinctive phenomenon in the way described above.

One might then ask: how precisely can this be true? That is a reasonable question, but it is one that I have already attempted to answer. The answer is the thesis that I have called simple compatibilism, and its defense turns essentially on options and their simplicity. In that sense, the perspective of agents and objects is no substitute for the more involved route to compatibilism pursued in Chap. 7. But it does help to understand why this debate has taken on the significance that it has and why, on the present view, we should respond to it somewhat equivocally. Agents are indeed a distinctive kind of being, fundamentally different from mere objects. And agents have a vast range of unexercised options, something that mere objects never have. And, at the same time, our world might be deterministic, with deterministic laws governing the agents as well as the mere objects. All of these things may be, and are, true together.

This is not a reconciliation with incompatibilism, or a granting that incompatibilism is true in some sense and false in another. Incompatibilism is false, and false in a profound way: it wrongly takes us to what we do not know, namely that determinism must be false, and to do so on grounds that are not grounds for knowing those things, namely reflections from the philosophy of agency. Incompatibilism is a violation of any sensible principle of philosophical humility, and it is thus that it can seem to its opponents to be not merely wrong but misguided.

Afterword: Of Agents and Objects 163

What then explains the enduring attraction of incompatibilism? I adduced some reasons in Chap. 7, but now we are in a position to state another. Incompatibilism expresses the true and important claims that there is a basic distinction between agents and non-agents. It also expresses many other claims, and in these it goes awry. But its core conviction is sound. This is why it can seem to its opponents not merely true but inevitably so.

Incompatibilism may be thought of, like many philosophical doctrines, as an impressionistic sketch of a landscape. It is not exactly right, and indeed it is literally false when laid against the world as we know it. But it aims to capture, however crudely and imperfectly, something deeply true. Accordingly, denying the accuracy of the sketch does not get things quite right either. This is what traditional compatibilists have aimed to do. What one ideally wants to do is to prescind from the details of the sketch and secure a point of view where one can see things a little more clearly.

The thought that beings like ourselves, agents, are fundamentally different from everything else that we encounter in our dealings with the world is a perennial one in philosophical thought. In this closing discussion, I have attempted simply to remind us of this distinction, and to indicate how much can be understood when we acknowledge it.

Bibliography

Breazeale, D. (2013). *Thinking Through the Wissenschaftslehre: Themes from Fichte's Early Philosophy*. Oxford University Press.

Chalmers, D. J. (1996). *The Conscious Mind: In Search of a Fundamental Theory*. Oxford University Press.

Dennett, D. C. (1984). *Elbow Room: The Varieties of Free Will Worth Wanting*. MIT Press.

Giubilini, A., & Levy, N. (2018). What in the World Is Collective Responsibility? *Dialectica, 72*(2), 191–217.

Harman, G. (1977). *The Nature of Morality: An Introduction to Ethics*. Oxford University Press.

Klaiman, M. H. (1991). *Grammatical Voice*. Cambridge University Press.

Makin, S. (2006). *Aristotle: Metaphysics Theta*. Oxford University Press.

Poulin-Dubois, D., Lepage, A., & Ferland, D. (1996). Infants' Concept of Animacy. *Cognitive Development, 11*(1), 19–36.

Reid, T. (1788/2011). *Essay on the Active Powers of Man*. Cambridge University Press.

Sartre, J. P. (1956). *Being and Nothingness: An Essay on Phenomenological Ontology* (H. E. Barnes, trans.) Routledge.

Scarantino, A. (2003). Affordances Explained. *Philosophy of Science, 70*(5), 949–961.

Schopenhauer, A. (1844/1966). *The World as Will and Representation* (E. F. J. Payne, Trans.). Dover Publications.

© The Author(s), under exclusive license to Springer Nature Switzerland AG 2022
J. T. Maier, *Options and Agency*, https://doi.org/10.1007/978-3-031-10243-1

166 Bibliography

Sider, T. (2011). *Writing the Book of the World.* Oxford University Press.

Skrbina, D. F. (2005). *Panpsychism in the West.* MIT Press.

Steward, H. (2012). *A Metaphysics for Freedom.* Oxford University Press.

van Inwagen, P. (1983). *An Essay on Free Will.* Oxford University Press.

van Inwagen, P. (1990). *Material Beings.* Cornell University Press.

Vihvelin, K. (2004). Free Will Demystified: A Dispositional Account. *Philosophical Topics, 32*(1/2), 427–450.

Wegner, D. M. (2002). *The Illusion of Conscious Will.* MIT Press.

Williams, B. A. O. (1992). *Shame and Necessity.* University of California Press.

Index[1]

A

Abilities
  dispositional analysis of ability, 68–70, 84, 86, 101
  general and specific abilities, 62
  Megarian view of ability, 60
'Able'
  ascription view of 'able,' 43–44
  general reading of 'able,' 50, 53, 62
  modal view of 'able,' 45–47
  specific reading of 'able,' 48
Affordances, 74–86, 74n12, 77n17, 88, 89, 91, 92, 94–96, 100, 158, 161n12
Agency, ix–xxviii, 1, 5, 6, 9–11, 12n11, 15, 16, 18–20, 25, 28, 30, 32, 34, 35, 37,
41–43, 54, 55, 63, 64, 67–68, 71, 72, 77, 90, 99, 101, 103, 106–112, 106n9, 111n13, 115–117, 119–123, 127, 130, 131, 134, 136, 139–141, 144, 145, 149, 150, 152–162, 154n4, 156n9, 156n10, 157n11, 161n12
Aristotle, xxvii, xxviin22, 14, 41, 42, 60, 100n1, 104, 157

B

Beebee, Helen, 144, 146, 146n3
Blame, xviii, xix, 5, 8, 13
Bratman, Michael, xv, 29, 29n20, 103

---

[1] Note: Page numbers followed by 'n' refer to notes.

© The Author(s), under exclusive license to Springer Nature Switzerland AG 2022
J. T. Maier, *Options and Agency*, https://doi.org/10.1007/978-3-031-10243-1

168 Index

C

'Can,' 6, 43n1, 53–57
Capacities, 92, 130
Causation, xi, xin3, 68n1, 83,
 83n24, 156, 160
Chalmers, David, xii, 35n32, 153
Choice situations, 4–6, 8, 37,
 128, 129
Compatibilism
 simple compatibilism, 15, 131,
 133–150, 160, 161n12, 162
 way of reduction, 123n6,
 124, 134
 way of sophistication, 123n6, 128
Consequence Argument, 10–13,
 13n12, 15, 142, 144, 146, 147
Control, xviii, xix, 5, 29–31, 30n22,
 49, 50, 53, 115, 145, 162
Counterfactuals, 20, 22, 23n7, 24,
 33, 33n27, 70, 78–80, 105,
 124, 124n7

D

Davidson, Donald, x–xii, xin2, xin3,
 xiin4, xiin5, xiv, xvi, xxi,
 xxin15, xxiiin18, xxiv, xxivn19,
 xxv, xxvii, xxviin22, 6, 7,
 102–104, 107, 109, 111, 125
Decision theory, 7, 9, 12, 32, 37, 99,
 103, 103n6, 128
Deliberation, 8, 24
Determinism, 3n2, 10–13, 10n7,
 10n9, 13n12, 32, 33, 33n26,
 33n28, 35n33, 87, 102, 104,
 107–109, 111, 111n13, 112,
 117–129, 131, 133, 138, 142,
 143, 161, 161n12, 162

Dispositional analyses
 dispositional analysis of belief, 84,
 85, 85n26
 dispositional analysis of color, 81,
 81n21, 82
Dispositions
 counterfactual analysis of
 dispositions, 79
 dispositional predicates,
 73–78, 73n9, 81, 85,
 88, 92, 158

F

Fischer, John Martin, xviii, 12, 128
Fixity
 fixity of the laws, 143, 144,
 146, 147
 fixity of the past, 143, 144, 147
Frankfurt, Harry, xvii, xxi, xxin13,
 8n6, 11, 11n10, 21,
 25, 71, 127
Free will, xvii–xxi, xxin14, 9–16,
 14n13, 115–117, 121, 122,
 149, 156n10, 159,
 160, 161n13

G

Genericity, 50–53
Gibson, James J., 74, 74n11, 75

H

Hume, David, 25n13, 100n1,
 101, 101n2, 101n3, 109,
 111, 111n14, 112, 116,
 129, 146

Index   169

I

Incompatibilism
  Formal Incompatibilism, 142,
    143, 147, 148
  Intuitive Incompatibilism,
    147, 148
Inheritance, 143–147
Intention, xiv, xv, 19n3, 22, 69, 102,
    103, 152

K

Kenny, Anthony, 27, 27n16, 28,
    28n19, 45
Kratzer, Angelika, xxvi, 33, 45,
    45n3, 56

L

Laws of nature, xviii, 106, 142, 143
Lewis, David, xvn8, xxivn19, xxvi,
    20, 23n7, 31, 31n23, 33,
    64, 93n33, 102,
    102n5, 146–147
Libertarianism, 120n4, 121

M

Martin, C.B., 79n19, 105, 105n7
Moral responsibility, xii–xv, xiiin7,
    xix–xxi, xxin14, xxiv, xxv, 8, 9,
    11–13, 12n11, 13n12, 14n13,
    15, 18, 22, 25, 100n1,
    127–130, 154, 154n4,
    159, 161n12

N

Naturalism, 133, 134
Nominalization, 58, 64

O

Options
  conditional analysis of options,
    20, 69, 70, 101, 101n2,
    139, 152
  modal analysis of options,
    26, 28, 45
  simple view of options, 31, 32,
    35, 36, 135

P

Performance Principle, 10n7, 33n26,
    36–37, 50, 99, 135–137, 139,
    140, 144
Phenomenal consciousness, 36,
    152, 153
Physicalism, 133, 134
Possibility
  agentive possibility, xiin4, xvi, 15,
    96, 99–112, 116, 134,
    157, 161n12
  epistemic possibility, 10n9,
    118–122, 120n4, 124, 127,
    128, 139, 148
Possibility Principle, 37–39, 56, 99,
    135–140, 144, 148
  Historical Possibility Principle,
    138–140, 142, 144
Possible worlds semantics, xxv,
    xxvi, 28, 157
Powers
  active powers, 15, 78, 87–92,
    90n31, 96, 158, 159
  passive powers, 15, 67–96,
    158, 159
Practical knowledge, 7
Propositions, xvii, xxii, xxvi, xxvii,
    19, 19n3, 26, 26n14, 28n18,
    30, 84, 103n6, 162

170 Index

Q
Quantum mechanics, 10, 10n8, 117
  Bohmian interpretation of
    quantum mechanics, 117

R
Reduction, 70, 100, 108, 122n5,
    123–127, 130, 131, 133, 149
Regret, ix, x, xiii, xxviii, 8, 8n5, 129
Reid, Thomas, 88–90, 89n29,
    89n30, 93, 151, 154, 157
Resentment, xiii, xiv, 8, 11, 129

S
Sartre, Jean-Paul, xvi, xxvii, 3n2, 157
Skepticism about the external world,
    xxin14, 118–120
Stalnaker, Robert, 20, 28n19

Steward, Helen, xiiin7, xvi, xxiv, xxv,
    10n7, 11, 18, 106–109,
    106n9, 112, 120, 127, 136,
    152, 161n12
Strawson, P.F., xiii–xvi
Supervenience, 35, 35n33, 36

V
Van Inwagen, Peter, xxn12, 33n28,
    117n2, 120n4, 122n5, 126,
    142, 142n2, 143, 146,
    151, 156n10
Vetter, Barbara, 43n1, 54n6, 105n8
Voice (grammatical), 154
Volition, 20, 23–25, 35, 70–72

W
Wallace, R. Jay, xn1, 11

Printed in the United States
by Baker & Taylor Publisher Services